PRAISE FOR
INNOVATION IS EVERYBODY'S BUSINESS

"The world is full of innovators—you just have to recognize and understand how to work with the best. Tamara's book will help you unlock the potential that innovation presents."
—Alex Goryachev, Managing Director,
Cisco Innovation Centers

"Lessons from neuroscience show that each individual's specific use and set-up of architecture and chemistry is the most individualistic 'fingerprints' we will ever own. Tamara eloquently deftly shows each of us how to access our own brand of innovation and how to unleash it on a world sorely in need of this wisdom."
—Scott G. Halford, *Wall Street Journal*
bestselling book, *Activate Your Brain*

"Tamara does an awesome job of giving tangible tools for anyone looking to become more innovative. She removes the intimidating stigma that can come with the thought of being innovative and shows how everyone plays a role in innovation. By sharing real world stories from a variety of companies, she shows how innovation can take place within any company of any size."
—Anthon⸝ ⸝atering

"In the 21st century, the ⸝ ⸝amara serves as a brilliant tour gu⸝ ⸝n—the world where we all now live, ⸝⸝⸝ ⸝⸝⸝⸝⸝⸝, and do our best work."
—Steve Woodruff, King of Clarity

"Tamara lays out exactly how to tap the competitive advantage hiding within all of us—our inner innovator and the ability to spark and foster a culture of innovation."

—Heather Kluter, Consumer Insights and
Brand Strategy Champion

"Finally an innovation book that provides clear direction, examples, and exercises that can be put into action immediately. Thanks for making innovation accessible, Tamara!"

—Wendy Winter, VP Business Leader, The Integer Group

"If you want to unleash thinking, creativity, innovation from every member of your team, read and do what's in this book."

—David Marquet, Captain of nuclear submarine,
USS Santa Fe, bestselling author of *Turn The Ship Around*

INNOVATION IS EVERYBODY'S BUSINESS

How to Ignite, Scale, and Sustain Innovation
for Competitive Edge

Tamara Ghandour

NICHOLAS BREALEY
PUBLISHING

BOSTON • LONDON

First published in 2020 by Nicholas Brealey Publishing
An imprint of John Murray Press

An Hachette UK company

24 23 22 21 20   1 2 3 4 5 6 7 8 9 10

A CIP catalogue record for this title is available from the British Library.

Library of Congress Control Number: 2019948851

ISBN 978-1-5293-9815-1
US eBook ISBN 978-1-529-39817-5
UK eBook ISBN 978-1-5293-9816-8

Printed and bound in the United States of America.

John Murray Press policy is to use papers that are natural, renewable, and recyclable products and made from wood grown in sustainable forests. The logging and manufacturing processes are expected to conform to the environmental regulations of the country of origin.

John Murray Press Ltd
Carmelite House
50 Victoria Embankment
London EC4Y 0DZ
Tel: 020 3122 6000

Nicholas Brealey Publishing
Hachette Book Group
53 State Street
Boston, MA 02109, USA
Tel: (617) 263 1834

www.nbuspublishing.com

To all of us, the Everyday Innovators, who wake up each morning seeking to have our voices heard and our contributions valued, those with the inner misfit who desperately seek to get out of the status-quo box we are often trapped in: ***Let's go make a dent in the world.***

Liam. Ari. Imma. Abba. Soupie.

Contents

Introduction

Ninety-six percent of your thoughts are repetitive.
That statistic blew my mind. Ninety-six percent of what you think is the same as it was the day before and the day before that.[1] It's hard to shift and adapt to changing times when your thoughts are stuck on continuous playback. Your mind is trapped in yesterday while the world around you zooms forward. Maybe that's why it feels so hard to adjust to change some days.

Let's make it easier. What you'll find on these pages is a mental framework for getting unstuck, like a gentle mental slap that shakes things up in your mind. Getting unstuck in your mind will shift your views and your behaviors to drastically transform your outcomes at work and in life and will unlock your natural ability to discover how to get off autopilot and step into your high-performing self.

This is not another tool to clutter your self-help toolbox but a new way of thinking. What I believe and have experienced is that having a mental framework helps to free up the most powerful tool you already have between your ears—your innovative mind. It's that simple.

Innovation is your greatest competitive advantage individually and in the teams you lead and are a member of. I'd like to encourage your success; I'd like to set the stage for what you *will* and *won't* find in this book and also present a challenge for you to participate in, ensuring you get the most out of your investment in yourself.

What You Will and Won't Find in This Book

#1: Bigwigs versus Everyday People and Companies

You won't find rearview mirror stories of Google or Apple or entire chapters dedicated to Elon Musk's morning routine or Beyoncé's mind-set. You won't find a lot of vice presidents of Spreading Enthusiasm or heads of Never-Been-Thought-of Ideas. Yes, these people are innovators I personally admire, but what they do is, for the most part, unattainable for the rest of us. I don't know about you, but I don't have Google's resources or Elon Musk's ability to risk it all to go to space or a job title that allows me to play all day.

You *will* find a lot of everyday people, like you and me, making an impact: people in large organizations fighting bureaucracy and igniting innovation; people on high-performing teams that drive innovation daily; people who crave to be the best at their work and be recognized for their contributions, or at least appreciated; people with titles like operations specialist, manager, entrepreneur, salesman, and janitor. These are the people who make innovation happen…and we are going to put a supercharged spotlight on them.

Often, when I refer to individuals who are implementing or learning about their Innovator characteristics, I indicate their two dominant styles with their names, e.g., Experiential Risk Taker (that's me). This helps us to begin thinking about ourselves and others in a new light. You'll learn more about these innovator characteristics throughout this book.

#2: Platitudes versus Actionable Takeaways

You won't find platitudes and hyperboles here. Many experts talk in grand and sweeping statements because, while they are good communicators, they lack the experience and depth to speak to specifics. You can't implement a platitude. You can't internalize a hyperbole. Those feel-good statements may get you all warm and fuzzy on the inside, but they don't get you very far on the outside. And, frankly, most of them are old and tired.

You will find real-world examples and actionable takeaways. You will find relatable stories I have collected over the years through my work with my company, LaunchStreet, including those from clients and interviews on the *Inside LaunchStreet* podcast. The stories shared here are from real conversations I've had across the globe with everyday people who come up to me after keynote addresses with real challenges and success stories. In some cases I changed the names and/ or generalized the industry to protect individuals in the story, while others have graciously shared who they are with you, the reader. In all cases, the details and experiences are real and recent. These are not something I read in a newspaper (unless it's historical) or collected from a case study. The exploits come from real-world Everyday Innovators. And, with those stories, you'll find relevant insights and actions you can apply immediately in your work and life.

#3: Process versus People

You will not find a lot of processes that are the "only" system you will ever need to innovate and win. The reality is you can implement all the processes you want, but if the people aren't on board, it doesn't matter. To create lasting behavior, change, and a culture shift, you need people involved. I know this because it's part of the reason leaders pick up the phone and call LaunchStreet for assistance.

Instead, you will find a mental model for how to be an Everyday Innovator. We combined the learnings from neuroscience, brain research, behavioral and social psychology, experience, and the tens of thousands of people across the globe who have taken our Innovation Quotient Edge (IQE) assessment. From that platform, we provide you with the mental framework to unlock your best self and the best in those around you. It will help you to understand how you innovate and perform at your peak and to create a scalable and sustainable culture of innovation around you, regardless of your title. The goal is to expand innovation through yourself and the people around you and avoid a process that attempts to put a square peg in a round hole.

#4: Personality Test versus Innovation Advantage

The IQE is not your typical personality test. While I love any tool that tells me more about who I am, what I find them lacking is application. I'm a Decider, and that's great, but what do I do with that information? How do I apply my Decider tendencies to gain an edge?

What you won't find with the IQE are paragraphs that stop with information about who you are. You probably know who you are already. It may be locked deep inside you, unused, but you know it's there.

What you will find with the IQE and this book, which is based on the information generated by IQE findings, is rich and insightful content, specifically about how you can become a high performer, add tremendous value to any project, and have a stronger voice in various environments—not just at work but in social groups, committees, and at home. There are many personality assessments out there, but the IQE is the only proprietary tool that explains how you can perform at your peak and gain competitive advantage by tapping the power of your unique style of innovation.

Read with Two Perspectives

Read and experiment with what you are learning...with two overlapping lenses.

Individual: Ultimately, this book is for and about you. Discovering your unique Everyday Innovator style is how you will be that high performer and have your ideas heard by those who matter. You'll be able to access on demand your never-ending wellspring of innovation superpowers.

Leader: Leadership isn't about a title; it's about influence. This book is going to help you be a stronger, more influential leader regardless of title. You will become a leader who is a catalyst for change, infusing innovation into the DNA of everything you and those around you do.

I urge you to read through the lens of a rock star innovator and envision how you can cause a massive ripple effect across your organization or community and ignite, scale, and sustain innovation.

Why Innovation Is Everybody's Business

All of us are capable of and responsible for innovation. Whether you run a solo business out of your home, are the night receptionist at a hotel, or are president of the company, innovation is your competitive advantage. Innovation comes from everyone and everywhere; those who think otherwise are myopic and destined to fail. The idea that innovation only happens when a single person is holed up alone in a garage is a false assumption. The concept that innovation only comes from certain places is false, too. In business today, whether you are part of a two-person or a 200,000-member team, everyone must unlock innovation to excel and win. Innovation means business, and everybody needs to be involved.

A Special Gift For YOU:

Given that you are reading this tells me you are someone who is already on your way to being an Everyday Innovator. It also tells me you have a growth mind-set. To reward you for taking the first step and encourage you on your journey, I'd like to offer you a gift. If you haven't yet purchased the IQE assessment to discover your full innovation superpowers, use this discount code to do so now. Having this knowledge will help you get the most out of the juicy content contained here.

The code is: IIEB.

If you already have the book and your IQE but missed accessing the online tool kit, use this same code, IIEB, for an extreme discount. The tool kit ensures you will learn methods to take advantage of opportunities to put your greatest asset into action; it's how you will stand out and shine. It's one thing to know who you are and keep it buried inside, but another to let it out and live it daily.

If you are ready to leap forward and create massive change, make sure you have the trifecta—IQE, book, and tool kit. It will change your game completely.

One Million Innovators Challenge

Did you know that 75 percent of people surveyed in an Adobe global benchmark study felt they were NOT living up to their creative potential?[2] That tells me 75 percent of people feel unfulfilled and are missing the sense of achievement that happens when you work toward and fulfill your unique purpose in this world.

My vision is to flip that. My big crazy dream is to unleash One Million Everyday Innovators into the world. Imagine the problems we could solve, the opportunities we'd create, and the sense of accomplishment and satisfaction we'd all feel. Think of the uniqueness and potential we'd unleash into the world.

Do you accept the challenge to become part of the One Million Everyday Innovators club and to be the change the world needs?

If you accept, let me know by posting to Instagram (@launchstreet), Facebook (@launchstreet) or Twitter (@launchstreet) or LinkedIn (@tamaraghandour) using the hashtag #1Minnovators. Share who you are and your unique Everyday Innovator style. You will be a part of an incredible community of innovators, and there is tremendous strength in connecting and sharing with one another.

"Remember, the question is not if you innovate, it's how you innovate, so let's get to it!"

—Tamara, Experiential Risk Taker

PART I:
DISCOVERING INNOVATION

Chapter 1

Discovering Innovation

I'll Never Forget Steve

I wanted nothing more than to work in advertising on Madison Avenue. In 1995, to me, all the great creative work originated on this magical street in the heart of Midtown Manhattan. When I graduated from the University of California at Berkeley, I bought a one-way ticket to the East Coast to make my advertising dreams come true. I landed a job as an account coordinator at the second largest global advertising agency. That meant I was the lowest on the organizational chart and was lucky to make copies or get coffee for my team.

One day, my boss pulled me into her office for what I would consider *big* news. She put me in charge of the annual meeting—the meeting where the creative strategy was set for the coming year. Everyone who touched the brand had to attend—the clients, the account management team that tracked the numbers, the team that ran the commercial production. Above all, the creative team would be there, with one creative in particular—Steve.

Steve had that creative mojo we all craved. He had multiple "aha" moments daily and wowed us with his creative brilliance. He'd start a sentence with "What if…" followed by a pause; we'd lean in, pens and notepads ready. My job was to pump everyone up to benefit from Steve's magical genius.

The big day arrives. It's a 9:00 a.m. start time, but I am there early. Steaming pots of coffee and containers of cream line the counter, markers and sticky notes of various colors litter the big conference table, and easel pads are set up at each end of the room…ready for Steve's brilliance.

8:45 a.m.: Clients and account management roll in. Energy is high as everyone grabs their first cup of coffee. No Steve. *But creatives are never early.*

9:00 a.m.: The rest of the advertising team arrives: Jill from accounting, Frank from media buy…. Everyone who touches the brand is chatting away with coffee in hand. Except for Steve. *But creatives are never on time.*

9:20 a.m.: The energy is fading, and people take their seats. No Steve. *But creatives are always late.*

9:45 a.m.: Everyone is sitting around the big conference table. The coffee is gone and people settle into their seats. The chatter dies down. No sign of Steve.

I'm instructed to find him, so I start dialing for dollars. I call the production room, the reception desk, every floor in the building. I finally reach him…at home. Why is he at home? I ask him, "Steve why aren't you here for the big meeting?"

He says, "Oh, I just wasn't feeling the mojo today, so we'll need to reschedule that." And he hung up! My short career flashes before my eyes. I look at the staring faces. I say, "Steve's not coming, sooooooo..."

A painful silence fills the room as we look around at each other, into space, at the floor. Then, the most amazing thing happens. Jill from accounting speaks up. She says, "I know I just look at the numbers, but I'm seeing this interesting pattern, and it gave me an idea." Then Frank from media buy says, "I'm seeing some trends with our competitors and it got me thinking about a few ideas." Before I knew it, the room was bubbling with innovative ideas— without Steve.

That experience set me on an obsessive path to better understand how we innovate. If given the ability and room to innovate, is everyone capable of being an innovator? And, if yes, why bestow special powers upon select people, like Steve, when anyone can unlock their own innovation superpowers?

In my 25+ years of work and research, the answer is crystal clear: Being innovative is built into our brains, our behaviors, and our environment; we just need to ignite it.

Let's find a new mental model to energize your amazing innovation.

Mental Model of Innovation

To understand a mental model of innovation, you must first understand what a mental model is.

Simply put, a mental model is the way in which you understand the world around you. It gives you a framework for how you think and how you perceive opportunities, challenges, and your beliefs and actions. I like to think of it as apps for your mind. The apps categorize and organize the content of your life, helping you make sense of it all. The apps you have on your phone are a reflection of how you see the world; you decide which ones to download. The same is true for your mental models. You decide the mental models through which you filter the world.

The beauty of mental models is they can be learned and unlearned. In fact, you have probably learned several in your lifetime and discarded a few along the way that didn't serve you. You might have different mental models for your exercise routine, your work ethos, your religious beliefs, and your relationships. Your mental model in those areas helps you move through your life with more efficiency and decisiveness. The effectiveness of your thinking and actions is directly related to the models in your head. Powerful and effective models will yield powerful and effective results. Weak and self-sabotaging models will yield the opposite.

Mental models come in many shapes and sizes. I have a colleague who always sees the worst in the world. No matter the topic of conversation, she is quick to point out the worst-case scenario or, at a minimum, tell you all the reasons why your idea won't work. Through her eyes, doom and gloom are right around the corner. Her mental model starts and categorizes the world around her from a negative vantage point. Hence, her beliefs about what's possible, her words, and her actions reflect this negative mental model. On the other side, I have another colleague who clearly has an opportunistic mental model of the world. For her, there's an opportunity everywhere she looks, even when we are stuck in rush hour bumper-to-bumper traffic with no way to get off the highway. She's the first to point out the strengths of your idea and share how you can take advantage of even the most frustrating situation.

What I propose is a powerful mental model of innovation—a model that accepts innovation as a powerful skill everyone embodies. Through our Everyday Innovator Styles, this model includes how you and those around you innovate and tap into unrealized potential. It's a model that puts the emphasis on the human side of innovation, not the processes and procedures that don't serve us. It's a mental model that I've seen transform the most unsuspecting people from average to outstanding innovators. You'll begin to see the world around you through a new lens. That lens will guide your beliefs, mind-set, and actions. Close your eyes and imagine for a moment what the world might look like through this lens. Are you seeing more opportunities, more paths to success? Yes!

This approach to the mental model breaks away from the traditional and ineffective models of the past that assume innovation is like rarefied air, elevating the innovation power to only a select few. The new and improved mental model works because it allows you take on the world through an innovation lens that expands how you see your situation, challenges, and opportunities. You gain the advantage.

I hope you'll discover how this mental model helps shift the results in your life and taps the power of innovation inside yourself and those around you. Create a model that doesn't limit you to an external process but an internal framework to help see the world and your place in it differently.

To accept this new model, you'll need to unlearn a few old models that may be holding you back.

Unlearn to Innovate

I'll never forget the moment my boss, a petite woman with a love of hierarchy, told me the projects a different team was working on were not my concern and dismissed the sales opportunity I discovered for them. As the most junior person in the company, my idea wasn't fully fleshed out, but I felt there was something to consider. Eager to present it in the all-team meeting, I raised my hand.

Partway through my explanation, my boss cut me off. I left that meeting feeling demoralized and detached when I should have felt valued and appreciated. I went the extra mile on something I didn't personally benefit from. For the next year, every time I had an idea, I shoved it deep down and didn't say a word. With that one experience, she made it clear that innovation was not my job responsibility or something I was capable of. Sadly, I believed her… for a short while.

Maybe you are not designated for innovation, but you have ideas. You've been frustrated and thought, *There has got to be a better way.* Have you been told to "stay the course" while others innovate? When you expressed your thoughts, were you encouraged or denigrated?

Most of us have experienced negative consequences, beginning in our childhood, for stepping out and thinking differently. The results of a study about creativity in the classroom found there was an inverse relationship between children ranked by teachers as their favorites and kids they considered creative.[1] Even though creativity was seen as highly valued by teachers in this study, creative students were their least favorite. Why do you suppose that was? Imagine 30+ kids in a classroom and the contingent of those who at times don't follow the rules, make up their own "right" answers, or require different learning approaches than the traditional memorization. Most often, they become disruptive and demanding… or disappear from the classroom.

You learn at an early age there may be punishment for thinking differently. You are encouraged and rewarded for finding the one right answer, not for the thinking process you go through to find that answer. When was the last time you were asked to share your thought process for making a decision, regardless of the impact of the decision? Or, do you remember when you were rewarded for the process you took to land the new client, or were you just rewarded (or punished) for the outcome?

Fear, Comfort, and Constraint

Over time, you believe that being an innovator isn't for you. You train yourself out of using your natural innovation strengths. They become weak, so when you do try to be innovative, you find it hard and exhausting, only validating that you aren't the innovative type. The internal chatter starts to hold you back, squelching the internal compass that keeps pointing you to a more innovative path, so you stop trying completely. It's been my experience that this manifests itself in three main reasons why you don't innovate even though you know it's possible and necessary.

Fear

Fear of failure, fear of looking stupid, fear of consequences, fear of the unknown...the fear list is long. What do you fear?

Fear is real. It's a primal response that your brain uses to keep you from getting hurt. Back in your caveman days, fear is what made you perk up when there was a rustle in the bushes. It could be a tiger coming to eat you. But in today's modern world, fear plays tricks on you. It keeps you tied to the status quo. Our minds manufacture false fears that unnecessarily put us into flight mode.

Almost five hundred years ago, Michel de Montaigne said it best: "My life has been filled with terrible misfortune; most of which never happened."

One study showed that 85 percent of what we worry about never comes to fruition.[2] That means most of what you fear—a negative response, an epic failure, being perceived as not worthy—never becomes a reality. This noise is your internal chatter holding you back. While the feeling of fear is very real, *what* we fear often is not.

Feelings of fear will never go away; it's hardwired into us. It's why you'll never hear me tell you to "dare to be fearless." It's unrealistic and impossible. It sets you up to fail, especially in the moment when fear creeps in. Then you think, *Forget it, I can't be fearless,* and you are right. Fear is part of the human design.

My goal is not to eliminate your fear but to unlock the innovative mind-set you need to embrace it and push through it.

Comfort

It's easier to stay where you are than to shift to something different. There is comfort in the familiar. Even if you don't like your current situation, at least you know it and it doesn't rock the boat.

Take a look at your work and life. How often do you choose to go to a restaurant simply because you could recite the menu back to the waitress without even having it placed on the table? Do you ever hold back from saying that innovative solution in a meeting because, if you say something, it might mean having to challenge yourself to do something new? Perhaps you think, *That will be too much work* or *I don't even know how I'd implement that.* That's comfort talking. It's a warm, supportive place that keeps you from growing into your full potential. Where are you letting comfort hold you back?

If you are part of the LaunchStreet community, you've probably seen the live 10-minute webcasts that I do randomly. The first one I ever did was on the topic of fear, comfort, and constraint. A girlfriend of mine, Holly, a grants and contracts manager who is an Imaginative Inquisitive, watched the recording and sent me this text:

I'm so bored in my role and ready for something new but **comfort** keeps me from applying to other positions. And we're currently without a supervisor so the team comes to me with all of the questions. I know most of them but I just recognized that I do a **little fear chatter** because I can hear them in their heads, like, why is she telling me what to do??

I think a lot of us can relate to her text: comfort and fear help us play it safe in subtle but powerful ways in life.

Constraint

Teena took a job at a large healthcare system. She even took a pay cut because she was excited to take her years of experience in marketing and strategy and apply those skills to something meaningful—exceptional healthcare for children. When she started her job, she had big dreams of implementing meaningful programs that would expand the reach of the hospital and children they served. She recognized that these new programs would require some adjustment in how the hospital thought about and managed the department, but she never shied away from a good challenge, and leadership gave her the verbal thumbs-up to innovate. It's why they hired her.

Teena immediately went to work. She worked quickly to present her ideas to her department. Her colleagues' immediate reactions were skeptical, but she expected some resistance to start. The initial resistance fueled her desire to keep going. But time and time again she found herself standing up against the brick walls of "not now," "too risky," and "not how we usually do it." The constraints of the system and the culture wouldn't budge and were starting to wear on her. She found herself less enthusiastic, not just for her new program ideas but work in general. She found herself continually thinking, *Why bother?* Every now and again, she'd bring up her innovative ideas to see if the tenor had changed, but she'd find herself facing those brick walls. Feeling totally beat down by the constraints, Teena left her position.

Some constraints can actually fuel innovation because they force you to think differently and do more with less, but continual, heavy constraints will snuff out innovation fast. They will wear down even the most resilient of us. Have you felt those constraints and found yourself in a "why bother" mind-set like Teena? It's hard to keep banging your head against that brick wall. You may start out with good intentions but get worn down and exhausted from trying to move forward without a shred of progress to feed your motivation.

I've seen massive brain drain, teams losing incredible people, because the constraints of the system sucked the innovative life out of them and they went in search of a system that would support their desire to innovate and grow.

Is your culture constraint- or opportunity-focused? Did Teena's story resonate with you because, even with all the talk of innovation, the culture and the system work against you?

"I didn't sign up to do remedial work. I signed up to innovate and help the business grow. They were more interested in toeing the line."

—Teena, Inquisitive Instinctual

If the constraints of the system you work in don't allow for anything but "how it's always been done," or decisions are made by determining how to avoid all risk, you are probably nodding your head right now. Constraints show up in unnecessary bureaucracy, complicated processes, and risk-averse cultures. Over time, these constraints feel like a heavy ball and chain weighing you down. What's the point of innovating if you are continually going to get shut down by the culture? Why spend your energy on innovating when the system forces you back into the box?

Sometimes constraints show up as self-created routines and boundaries. Why shake up your routine when it's clearly working for you? Why move the boundaries if you can see them clearly?

A few paragraphs up, I asked if you continually go to the same restaurants as a sign of comfort. My kids and I have our favorite weekend go-to restaurant. It's a dingy Greek diner we've been eating Saturday lunches at since the kids were in highchairs. We know the menu, the waitstaff, and the perfect times to go when it's not too busy. One Saturday, my kids just weren't feeling the standby gyro salad.

My oldest said to me, "Hey, let's try that new restaurant down the street. It looks interesting."

I responded with a shocking amount of resistance. I said, "No, let's just do the usual. At least we know it's going to be good, and I don't want to take the risk of a bad lunch."

My oldest responded, "Is one bad lunch really a big risk, Mom?"

I suddenly realized what I was doing. I was staying in my warm, soft, fuzzy comfort zone over one simple lunch! My fear chatter made the risk of a possibly bad meal outweigh my ability to try something new. And the Saturday routine I loved so much had turned into a self-imposed constraint. Was I doing that in other aspects of my life, my work? Are you doing that?

We went to the new restaurant. While it wasn't knock-your-socks-off delicious, it was good enough. That conversation with my kids about where to eat lunch made me realize how often we let fear, comfort, and constraint override taking a more innovative path. We attach *perceived* risk and consequences to it. We let that chatter dictate what we say, do, and believe.

I can't eliminate the chatter in your head, but I can help you put it in its place. The first step in showing your chatter who's really in charge is identifying how it shows up for you.

The Challenge

If you are open to challenging yourself (fingers crossed you say yes), I have an exercise for you to do. This exercise will bring to the surface your fears, your need to feel comfortable, and even the constraints you may be feeling. Don't worry, while it's short and fun to do, the "ahas" that come from it are very powerful. Here's the thing: to get the benefits of this exercise, you can't just read it, you have to do it. Believe me, the thousands of people who have done it are glad they did. It's like how I feel about running—sucks while I'm doing it, but I'm extremely glad I did it when it's over. This only takes five minutes and requires zero physical exertion—just a desire to improve.

If you are alone, do this in a busy café. If you are with a team, do this in your next meeting.

First, I want you to identify someone you don't know (easy to do in a café) or know the least (possible in your next meeting). Make sure you can see their face from your vantage point.

Then, pull out a blank piece of paper and a pen. Give yourself 90 seconds to draw that person. Do not tell them what you are doing.

Finally, I want you to show your drawing to them. I know. Horrifying, right?!

I've done this exercise several hundred times with teams as small as 10 and with groups as large as a few thousand. What I love about it is that all your deepest, darkest fears show up in this short experiment: fear of your own inadequacies as you try doing something outside your comfort zone; fear of looking stupid as you show them your drawing; fear of the judgment that comes with stepping out of what you know works.

I love how this exercise also shows how many layers of judgment you put on your own ideas before you even get them out into the world. With the sharing part of this exercise, those judgments show up in fear statements like "I failed art" and "I'm so sorry." Those thoughts are trying to keep you in your comfort zone. Some people will even hide their drawings so they don't have to go through what they think is the pain of showing their hideous attempt to draw to someone who is obviously going to ridicule them for their poor performance; better to stay totally complacent.

In doing that, you shut yourself and your innovative mind down. How do you expect to unlock your greatest competitive advantage, your ability to innovate, and create breakthrough results if you let fear and comfort take over and shut yourself down before your ideas even see the light of day? How are you going to thrive in today's competitive world if your own constrained thinking holds you back from moving forward?

You are your own worst critic and the root of most of the fear— not the boss or client or family member you are intimidated by. It's Y…O…U!

In work, this often shows up in fear chatter in your mind like, *They'll never go for it, It will never work, Who am I to have this idea when it's not even my area of responsibility,* or *There must be a good reason no one has thought of this before, so never mind.*

After you've done the exercise, take inventory on the experience by answering these questions:

Question #1: When you read the exercise description, did you think *that's exciting* or *that's horrifying*? And why?

Question #2: What emotions did you experience while doing the exercise? While drawing someone? When showing it to a stranger? After showing it to a stranger?

Question #3: What did you learn about your own relationship with fear, comfort, or constraint in doing this exercise?

Question #4: In what situations do you hold yourself back, and where do you leap into things across your work and life?

Question #5: **If you decided to do this exercise, what made you do it?**

Did your answer include: *Because I wanted to see if it was as awkward as it is for others; because I love trying things that scare me; I'm always up for a challenge; I leap and then think*? Or something else? I ask this very basic question because your answer will provide tremendous insight into who you are and how you tackle work and life. While you are on the front end of unlocking your innovation advantage, how you responded to this exercise helps you identify your internal chatter. When we layer on your Everyday Innovator style, you'll be unstoppable.

If you decided not to do this exercise, which excuse did you use? Hint: your answer might include: *I'll read everything first and go back and do it later; I can't draw; no one will know I did or didn't do it anyway; That's way too uncomfortable for me.* If answering why you decided to skip the exercise is uncomfortable for you, don't beat yourself up about it. We are only at the beginning, and this is a very insightful start to your journey in unlocking your innovation super-powers. Do not feel inadequate or called out for this. Rather, I want you to feel empowered because you just gained some deep insights into what might be a pattern holding you back in your work and home life. You now know how to recognize it, and this book will give you the framework for overcoming it and becoming unstoppable.

What's Holding You Back?

Before reading further, I encourage you to take a moment to address the attitudes holding you back. Don't settle for surface answers; dig deep. Sometimes what's holding you back is obvious, and other times it's so insidious you don't realize it's happening, like a frog in boiling water. Try to take a step back and look in from the outside.

You can't tap into your greatest asset—your innovative mind— if there is an invisible barrier between you and the world around you shutting it down. It's time to be the rock star innovator you were meant to be.

To be a rock star innovator, you first need to become aware of the world you are dealing with and learn how to address change.

Chapter 2

Irrelevancy Lurks around the Corner

Seize Change

When faced with change, you have two choices: you can fight it or you can embrace it.

Samantha was the executive director of the Statewide Media Association at the exact moment in history when the media landscape was drastically changing. The print press was fighting for relevancy, digital content was taking over, and the everyday blogger had become daily sources of information. The newspaper industry was at odds with the change in the world. If you are slightly experienced (aka over 40), you remember the days when opening up your front door to grab the oversize Sunday paper was a big deal. Then Twitter came onto the scene and, suddenly, anyone could communicate in 140 characters or fewer, the 24-hour news cycle created instant access to everything going on anywhere in the world. Sites like the HuffPo and Reddit meant you didn't need to be a journalist to share your opinions with the world.

As with any industry at the tipping point of change, a few brave souls see change as an opportunity to seize new ground while the majority flounder to keep the old way of life. Unfortunately, the ones who fight the hardest are usually the ones who lose the most.

In a meeting with heads of newspaper agencies, Samantha said to the group, "Tradition is what got us here, but convention is what is holding us back." Samantha recognized that tradition made them successful, but in today's ever-changing world, fighting the change by holding on to old conventions was a fast path to irrelevancy.

As a Futuristic Risk Taker, Samantha has her eye to the future and understands it takes bold thinking and a willingness to get uncomfortable to chart a new path to success.

The mistake I see people make when it comes to change is holding on for dear life to old ways of thinking. Innovation doesn't come from fighting change, it comes from grabbing it by the horns and making it your biggest asset. You don't need to be some wild maverick to do so. Anyone can embrace change.

Libraries are a good example for the transition of then to now. Traditionally, libraries are a place where you go to get "shushed" for speaking above a whisper. You walk in quietly, try to navigate the Dewey Decimal Classification system, check out a few books, and leave. While libraries have stayed relatively the same, the world around them has not. Google is now our go-to source for any and all information. If someone asks you a question you don't know the answer to, what do you say? "Google it." Wikipedia, the online collaborative encyclopedia, is often the first option that comes up when you google something. Access to this content, from across the globe, fits in your front pocket. I ask you, does a big building that warehouses books and tells you "Please be quiet" if you laugh out loud sound relevant? Of course not.

If libraries try unwillingly to change with the times, they might ask, *How do we make our warehouse of books relevant?* It's the wrong question and resists the inevitable.

On the other hand, Anythink Libraries is a library system in metro Colorado that considered a different question. Pam Sandlian-Smith, as director of the libraries and a Fluid Collaborative, sought to take the chaos that the change was creating and swirl it around to create an innovative solution. Stacie Lidden, director of innovation and brand strategies at the libraries and a Collaborative Futuristic, pulled from her many experiences and insights and looked to the future to create new possibilities. Together they asked, *How do we seize change and turn it into something meaningful?* When they took on leadership, their libraries were the lowest funded per capita in the state of Colorado, and resources were not at their fingertips. Again, they saw this as part of the change they needed to harness. As the name suggests, it's less a library and more of a center of discovery for the communities they serve. Their librarians are called "wranglers," and when you walk through the door you can feel the excitement. More important, you can hear it. There are teenagers, families, and adults everywhere—and they are talking. In fact, their wranglers wear T-shirts that say "Shhh is a four-letter word." They eliminated the Dewey Decimal System in favor of organizing books the way you might find them in an actual bookstore—category, title, author. Best of all, they have no more late fees. They might have Ping-Pong tables, discovery stations, classes, technology, fireplaces, and a huge outdoor common area. Even teenagers flock to their libraries after school.

It would have been easy for Anythink to go down fighting the wrong fight and feel justified doing so. They could have said, "The problem is the kids these days that spend all their time staring at a small screen." Fortunately for everyone, they didn't. Instead, they said, "How do we take this media-savvy, Insta-Google generation and speak to their needs?" They harnessed the heck out of change. Now they are a beacon for innovation and success, elevating the entire library industry along with them.

Pam, Stacie, and their teams at Anythink Libraries are a great example of what's possible when you embrace change.

I believe there are two main reasons we choose to deny or fear change instead of embracing it like Stacie and Pam.

#1: Longevity Preference

You generally have a natural bias toward longevity. In one study, participants found a piece of art painted in 1905 more appealing to look at than the same piece of art described as having been painted in 2005.[1] In a more delicious study, participants were given a piece of European chocolate. One set of participants was told the chocolate brand had been founded three years ago; the other set was told the brand had been sold in its region of origin for 73 years. Can you guess which piece of chocolate they liked better? That's right, the one described as being made by a 73-year-old brand, even though it was the exact same chocolate.[2]

Humans prefer things we think have been around for longer. It could be why transferring from the old database to the new one seems so hard. It's not just that you have to learn how the new dashboards work; it's that you innately attached "good" and "worthy" identities with the old system simply because it had been around a while. Your mind sees it as proven. It's why you may have an adverse reaction to a new idea simply because it's new. It's an unconscious filter in your brain telling you new is "bad" and old is "good." As you can imagine, it's hard to innovate with a bias toward familiar. As you begin to unlock your innovative mind and recognize some of these biases and patterns, you'll begin to over-come them. It's not that hard. Notice your reaction to new things and question your preferences before making a decision about how to react.

#2: Fear of Being Changed

It's been my experience that people don't fear change; what they actually fear is *being* changed. Chip and Dan Heath's book *Switch* does a fantastic job delving deeper into this distinction. For our purposes, let me highlight why this distinction matters to you. If you can recognize how much control you have over what you do with the change happening around you, the fear will dissipate. When you recognize that change is something you can harness, you'll begin to embrace it. Deep down, fear of change comes from fear of lack of control. When I suggest you control and recognize change, I'm not saying you can control it if your company decides to reorganize or if a new technology comes out that makes what you are doing seem outdated. What you can control is what you do with that change. You can control if you see those events as moments to throw in the towel or find the opportunity.

Think about the last time you had to deal with change. It could be anything from a change in your exercise routine to a shift in job responsibilities or a new competitive threat that meant chang-ing your business flow. Whatever it was, how did it make you feel? Did the little voice in your head get excited to take a new path or did it make you stiffen up with resistance? Did the little voice in your head chatter on about how this is going to change how you do things? More often than not, your resistance to change is less about the change itself and more about how you think it's going to change you. Move on; it's time to get rid of that perspective and voice.

There are a lot of changes and pressures being hurled at you every day, so let's recognize them for what they are—an opportunity to seize change.

The Four Headwinds of Change

Open up any news app and you'll read about the latest company disrupted and out of business: Blockbuster, Sears, Pan Am Airlines, BlackBerry, Circuit City.... The tombstone list will increase between the time I write this book and the time you read it. In business, we talk about these failed companies from the rearview mirror as abstract case studies, big data presentations with beautiful graphs and charts and high-level trend reports. We hold them up as lessons for what not to do.

In fact, the average lifespan of an S&P 500 company has dropped from 61 years in 1958 to what McKinsey & Company believes will be 18 years in 2027.[3] You'll live longer than most of the businesses and brands you currently use in your life.

More than that, you will probably be one of the hundreds of thousands, if not millions, of people affected by changes in businesses. People like you and me are deeply impacted by the irrelevancy that lurks around the corner.

An informal study with my clients and colleagues over the past couple of years reveals four key areas that impact us and highlight the necessity of upping our ability to innovate. When asked "What keeps you up at night?," it wasn't the big data and statistics but the elements of change to our business environment that impact us on a deeper and more personal level.

#1: Accelerated Rate of Change

Change has always existed. If you ask your parents or grandparents if they lived through a time of change, they'll give you a resounding yes. What's different now is the unbelievable rate of change. Technology is changing faster than our cognitive ability to change with it, so we are truly always behind.[4] You go to bed with one concept for how the world works and wake up to another. As one client told me, "I'm operating on all burners and I'm still in chase mode."

How has the superspeed of change affected your ability to play at a high performance level?

#2: Continuous Disruption

Jason, the vice president at a regional bank, described it like this: "In the old days you'd have one major disruption that was like one big earthquake. The ground would shake for everyone, we'd all wait for the dust to settle, figure out the new normal, and then move forward together. Now there are dozens of microdisruptions coming at me every day. The ground is continually shaking, so, instead of figuring out how to operate in the new normal, I have to figure out how to stabilize when things are always shaking and moving. I'm always off balance."

Disruption is ever present in big and small ways across every aspect of our lives. It can hit us at any time, especially when we least expect it.

I found myself in the line at a rental car agency at the airport. I'm behind two gentlemen discussing their important new business pitch when abruptly one says to the other, "I literally can't wait for someone to disrupt this entire rental car business. The way it works is archaic." I'm assuming something has gone horribly wrong with his rental car. I'm now gearing up for an epic battle where he goes to the counter and lets the poor unsuspecting soul have it, the supervisor has to be called out, and the full offense battle begins.

He's eventually called up to the counter. I roll up my sleeves and inch closer so I have a front row seat to the fight. I'm nervous with anticipation. The person behind the counter politely types on the keyboard; he answers a few questions about extra insurance and prepaid gas; she gives him his keys and smiles. He says thank you, and the pair go on their way.

Where's the frustration and rage? Isn't he the same person who said he wanted this whole industry to die and be reborn anew?

The much-anticipated rage wasn't there because, like most of us, he doesn't care enough to say something. In fact, he expects some innovator to come in and disrupt the business, as Uber did to the taxi companies. And, with every business disruption, there is a people disruption.

With short business cycles, disruption has become an expectation for the brands we buy and the jobs we are tasked to complete. We no longer expect the businesses we buy from or the brands we use to be around forever. We don't even expect the jobs we do to last. The challenge is, while we may encourage and even applaud disruption, we also recognize its power to come for *us* at any moment. With every disruption, big and small, comes a change in how we as individuals have to operate as well.

Disruption can take you by surprise *if* you aren't the one doing the disrupting. This is why it's so important to embrace and harness change so you can avoid being surprised and maintain a sense of control.

It's how you retain your balance in an ever-shifting world.

#3: Crowded Playing Field

The exciting news is that the barriers to business are the lowest they've ever been. The bad news is that the playing field is more crowded than ever before. Your competition is fierce and growing at the business and personal levels.

At the business level, you are competing with everyone and everything. No matter what business you are in, your competitive set includes everyone with whom your customers come into contact. For example, if you work at a yoga studio franchise, you aren't just competing against other yoga-style studios, you are competing against every wellness option available to that customer: spin classes, functional fitness classes, a full gym, virtual classes like Peloton, highly specific programs like Orange Theory, going for a walk with your dog, online programs by Instagram fitness stars, doing nothing... the list goes on. And on top of that, you are now being compared to every business your customer has ever interacted with. If you can't respond to me instantly as someone from Zappos does or remember my name as my neighborhood coffee shop does, you are not living up to your customers' expectations.

Marjorie Burnam, the executive director of SOCAP International, the leading national customer service association, said it best, "You are only as good as your customer's last experience with someone else."

As a Fluid Tweaker, Marjorie recognizes that competition and the overall playing field are packed. To stand out, you need to differentiate yourself from the world of choices, and there are lots of them.

As my Inside LaunchStreet podcast guest and Experiential Futuristic innovator Steve Woodruff said to me, "We all have the same fierce competitor—noise."

Therefore, doing your job the way you've always done it won't cut it. All you'll be doing is adding to the noise, and that won't get the results you need to stay relevant.

"Better" doesn't cut it in today's cutthroat world. To win you have to be different. The pressure to create differentiation then gets pushed down across organizations to you, where it affects how your work is perceived and valued.

On a personal level, you are not only being judged against the bullet points in your job description, you are being compared with how everyone else in your organization performs and how the technology handles that work, and you're being pitted against people spotlighted in magazines for their breakthrough thinking. Five generations of people are squeezed into the workforce competing to be the ones who stand out.[5] As much as I hate to write this, the hard truth is that your shelf life as an employee or entrepreneur is shorter than ever if you aren't adapting and innovating.

The CEO of IBM, Ginni Rometty, even coined a term, "new collar," to describe the workforce that is needed in today's business environment.[6] Unlike the old descriptors of blue collar and white collar, which describes the textbook skills, certifications, and experience needed to complete a job, "new collar" describes the ability for creative problem solving, critical thinking, and adapting to change. In essence, it's your ability to be innovative.

The pressure that comes from a crowded playing field will make you feel like you are working in a pressure cooker all day long.

#4: Technology & AI

In the 1980s and '90s, the big fear was outsourcing of jobs. Today, it's a robot taking over your job. You see it everywhere, from checkout stands at the grocery store, minimizing the need for clerks; smart home devices that listen to you, do your bidding, and tell you what you want and need; or technology that manages scheduling and day-to-day tasks. There isn't an industry immune from the tech takeover.

A study done by McKinsey & Company in 2017 found that for six out of 10 jobs, 30 percent of the tasks for that job are automatable.[7] That number is increasing in jobs affected and work completed. It prompts many people to ask themselves, *How do I add value if technology can do my job?* The future has arrived and it's giving lots of us insomnia.

What's Your Wind of Change?

What keeps you up at night? (I hope it's reading this book!...LOL)

Whatever your winds of change include, you live under a constant threat of irrelevancy. Like a lump of coal that needs intense pressure to transform into a sparkling diamond, the pressure to change can turn into an opportunity to succeed.

Embrace the credo that innovation is everybody's business, especially yours.

Winds of Change Carry Opportunity

Greg is tall and lanky. He leans into me, almost bending at the waist, so that no one at the conference will hear his next comments. What he says to me blows my mind, "Tamara, in five, maybe 10 years, the accounting degree won't even exist. Technology can now do what I studied four years to master. Tech can do it faster and better than me."

With wide eyes I respond, "Why are we here talking innovation then? Let's just throw in the towel and go get coffee." I was half serious, half joking, not sure how to respond to his blunt statement.

He went on to explain, "Tamara, this is where it gets good. Now that technology can do all the baseline work, I am free to really use my mind. I can provide way more value being innovative and strategic than I can crunching numbers. If we harness this shift, it's going to create a lot of opportunity for me, for all three hundred accounting management people in this room. Change is opportunity."

You can fight, deny, or resist change, or you can be like Greg and embrace it, see it for what it really is—an opportunity to innovate.

To truly unlock the mind-set of opportunity, let's move innovation from something subjective and hypothetical to something real and tangible you can engage in daily.

Chapter 3

Real & Tangible Innovation

The Four Traps of Certainty

To unlock your ability to innovate, it's important to remove the traps that become self-sabotaging behaviors. These traps state that innovation is for certain people, certain times, certain segments and processes of business. It is not. Innovation is for everyone and every aspect of life.

Fortunately, when you recognize the traps, you can easily break free from their hold and become the Everyday Innovator you were always meant to be.

Trap #1—Certain People

The Richard Bransons, J. K. Rowlings, Elon Musks, Lady Gagas, and Steven Spielbergs of the world are clearly the innovative ones. The rest of us should glorify and mimic their morning routines, self-talk, and dress codes. If we are lucky, we'll be one-hundredth of a percent as innovative as they are. Let's put them on a pedestal, worship them, and study them.

You probably know someone right now who's treated this way. Maybe it's someone named Helena, with her purple highlights and funky glasses, who is bestowed with the great gift of imagination and creativity. Her days are filled with "aha" moments and brilliant insights. If you're lucky, perhaps you are standing close to her while she says something magical that you can execute.

I'm not sure where this narrative of the "select few" came from, but it's dead wrong. I hear it time and time again when people are assessing themselves. Have you ever caught yourself saying something like "Oh, I'm not innovative; that's for Helena," or "I don't have a creative bone in my body," or "If only I were more innovative like Josh"?

I also see this narrative in organizations that anoint a select few as innovator. Perhaps it's a small department, team, or committee that gets to go off and innovate while the rest of us are told to keep our heads down and get our jobs done. As much as I admire incredible people like Helena and the famous innovators I mentioned above who provide massive contributions to the world, they aren't the only ones who are capable of innovation.

As an individual, when you abdicate innovation to someone else, you are telling your brain not to bother. It becomes a
self-fulfilling prophecy. Being innovative becomes harder because
you made it so. It's like bullying your brain into shutting down
one of its greatest natural skills. Occasionally, it'll pop up with
innovative ideas, but you shut it down, and eventually your brain
acquiesces to your commands and stops activating that incredible
natural talent. It's the brain acting as a muscle concept we discuss
in more depth in Chapter 4, The Science of Innovation. Much like
your self-confidence, your brain needs validation.

In organizations, when teams or a select few are given special
powers and responsibilities, the rest of the organization suffers a
blow. The decision makers are telling the unanointed that they
don't have a voice in the growth of the organization. Nothing
is more demotivating than feeling like your contributions aren't
needed or valued. It hurts on a personal level.

Frankly, I've never understood why organizations would only
want to tap the power of six or 14 people when they could tap the
power of all 300; 3,000; or 300,000 employees. You aren't paying
your team to keep their heads down. You are paying them to help
you grow and thrive as a business. If you don't have that expectation, you're missing countless opportunities.

Laura looked perplexed during my innovation workshop. At
the break she came up to share her concern. She said, "I work at
a national law firm. In an effort to be more innovative, leadership
designed a cross-functional committee. That committee is going
to look across the company, figure out where we can innovate, and
then report back to us the changes we need to make. Do you think
that's a good idea?"

I responded to her question with another question: "How

does that make you feel?" Her body visibly sucked inward as she answered, "It makes me feel pretty bad. It's like they are telling me my ideas don't matter, yet I'm here thinking about my work all the time. I feel unmotivated and more disengaged than ever before. Why doesn't my voice count, too?"

Talk about falling deep into the Certain People trap. Laura is out there thinking about her job 24/7. Why wouldn't you want to put innovation in her hands? The most innovative and meaningful business opportunities often come from the most everyday sources—the ones thinking about their work day in and day out.

Gunpei Yokoi was a janitor at Nintendo. Not a programmer, he didn't have a computer science degree. What he did have was an innovator's mind-set. Yokoi, the janitor, is responsible for some of Nintendo's biggest successes, like the Gameboy and Donkey Kong.[1] Innovation is everybody's business—up, down, and sideways on the organizational ladder.

Trap #2—Certain Times

Usually it's a 3:00 p.m. brainstorm with scented markers and a blank easel pad. The person leading the meeting warms you up with some ridiculous question that is supposed to spark new ideas. Maybe you've heard it before: "If you could be any animal in the jungle, what would you be and why?"

In the allotted one-hour time frame of the meeting, you are

supposed to fill up a blank easel pad with brilliant innovation. You walk out of the conference room and it's back to business as usual. No more innovation until the next specifically scheduled time, usually a couple of weeks or months later.

Let's do the math. In a 40-hour work week, one out of 40 hours, or 2.5 percent is all you get for innovative thinking. The remaining 39 hours, or 97.5 percent of your week, is status quo. Don't you dare do any critical thinking or creative problem-solving in those hours! That's only for 3:00 p.m. brainstorms. In the math alone, you can see that point-in-time innovation makes no sense.

The best innovation doesn't happen at the 3:00 p.m. brainstorm; it happens when you are immersed in your work, when you experience a frustrating task or are simply going about your day. Be prepared for it to happen 24/7.

Trap #3—Certain Segments

It's what we see on magazine covers. A young hotshot has a hypercool technology that is going to change the world. Or it's a radical thinker in a faded T-shirt who has created a product that is going to disrupt the titans of industry. Yes, those are definitely innovative, and I encourage anyone with the gumption to go after those blue skies to do so. But the latest technology or disruptive product isn't the only way to define innovation. The truth is that innovation can happen anywhere and everywhere. In fact, some of the best innovation happens in the departments you would least expect, in places that aren't sexy and/or glamorous or departments that face customers, but the impact is just as great.

Some of my most rewarding work has been done by teams such as project management, internal auditing, the IT department, and sales. And the impact they create from innovating is just as real and lasting as the latest product or technology.

Trap #4—Certain Processes

If you work for a progressive-minded company, you may have heard something like this before:

"We have a new innovation initiative we are rolling out over the next couple of months."

Just reading that sentence can generate the heebie-jeebies if initiative fatigue has set in. *Don't we have enough processes and systems to follow?* I'm not suggesting companies and their employees don't need some structure, but the focus on a singular process to drive and scale innovation is often a failed one.

I don't care how good your processes are, or if they are proven and tested, or if they are the flavor of the month in Silicon Valley, they won't work if process is your starting point for innovation. Why? Because process-first innovation always fails. It lacks the critical component for success—people. I've seen millions of dollars and personal energy wasted on innovation initiatives that never go anywhere. They get stalled and have a negative effect when they become just another latest fad imposed on teams by leadership. Employees often view these types of initiatives with an extreme eye roll and a wait-it-out mentality.

Initiative fatigue was demonstrated in a recent experience with the latest collaboration software I tried to implement. Everyone on my team is juggling a lot of responsibilities, and sometimes they get tunnel vision. I heard about this new, shiny collaboration system for teams on a business podcast and got excited. I downloaded the software, spent 20 minutes inputting our information, another 20 minutes launching this new save-all system with my team, closed it out so we could get on a conference call, and then barely touched it again. Maybe one person on my team used it... once. It only took 40 minutes for us to go from all-in to all-out—another failed effort.

I've witnessed leaders glom on to the latest innovation system or technology, believing it will be the save-all they've been lacking. However, behaviors start and scale with *people,* not systems.

A Definition of Innovation You Can Use

Now that you've identified and removed the innovation traps, let's get on the same page about what real and tangible innovation looks like. This isn't the textbook definition; rather, it's a foundation built on years of experience, failures, and successes.

First, this definition transforms innovation from a point-in-time exercise to a mind-set. Second, it democratizes innovation, taking it out of the silos and hands of special people and into the hands of everyone.

INNOVATION: Thinking differently about what's right in front of you to create an advantage.

That's *real* innovation. Anyone can do it; it happens daily and you don't need to build an initiative around it.

Let's break it down:

Thinking differently: using the power of your innovative mind to shift your perspective, take a new path, adjust your ideas, question your decisions, use your innovative powers to adapt and adjust.

...about what's right in front of you: your real-world constraints, opportunities, resources, time, people, money, etc.; the work on your desk, the task at hand—not just the blue skies but the realities you face and are trying to tackle every day. We all have these "issues," so walking away from them and not acknowledging the realities of your world makes no sense and won't get you very far. Plus, there's so much room for tiny and breakthrough innovation right in front of you, why bother looking elsewhere?

...to create an advantage: a more efficient process, a breakthrough product, a more productive way to work, an edge on the competition, a more meaningful solution, a way to leverage change. As the definition implies, this is the point where you create something favorable to your success, interest, or desired end.

I can't tell you the number of times I've led a blue skies project only to have it go nowhere because when we brought our brilliant ideas back to the real world, they fizzled. Once I recognized the pattern and connected what was right in front of me with thinking big and disruptive, I began to see results. Don't ignore the opportunities right in front of you. You'll get to that new-to-the-world idea by starting right where you are today.

Creativity versus Innovation

What comes to mind when you think of the words *creativity* and *innovation*?

If you ask 10 people in a room to define either word, you'll get 10 different answers, each with its own connotations and baggage. Particularly in the business world, creativity is often associated with artistic endeavors like drawing, dancing, or even clever stand-up comedy. Or it's showcased with clever marketing or product packaging.

When I Googled "definition of creativity," the first result indicated it was "the use of the imagination or original ideas, especially in the production of an artistic work."

Innovation, on the other hand, isn't limited to imagination or original ideas, and it's definitely not restricted to the pursuit of artistic outcomes. Innovation is about all the ways you think differently, the pursuit of elevating and differentiating everything you do.

I've also found the word *innovation* to feel more inclusive than *creativity*. Creative people often look and act a certain way, but anyone can be innovative.

I suggest that, like the thousands of people in the One Million Innovators Club, you embrace the definition of innovation that ignites, scales, and sustains innovation inside you and the people you are surrounded by.

Rearranging how you think about innovation can make all the difference.

Rearranging the Box You Have

I hate the phrase "outside the box." To me, it implies you have to completely walk away from all your realities. It's unnecessary and unrealistic. It's been my experience that, instead of finding it inspiring when it's given as a command from leadership, it actually shuts people down. Where do you even look? What do you do when you have to go back to the box you work in?

I'd like to suggest you forget "outside the box" and simply seek to rearrange the box you have. My first experience with the "box" came when I was a teenager.

When I was 14, I loved fashion. It was the 1980s, so the fashion wasn't particularly functional or appealing, but I didn't know any better at the time. Every dollar I made that summer at my job at the miniature golf place went to filling my closet with new clothing. My closet spilled over with off-the-shoulder sweaters, pegged pants, and jelly shoes. In typical teenage girl fashion, my girlfriends would come over on the weekends to borrow the latest outfits. It didn't matter what we bought, we wanted to wear what our girlfriends had in their closets.

One day, as my friend Jill rummaged through my clothes, I realized something: My closet was full of opportunity. When Jill emerged from my closet with the latest shirt with shoulder pads and pegged pants on her arm, I said, "You can rent those for two dollars." That day, in a 14-year-old's bedroom, a rental business emerged. I even developed a rate card: a dollar for tops, two for pants, and 50 cents for scrunchies. The category in which I made the most money? Late fees.

Looking back, what I did that summer was think differently about what was right in front of me—Jill and a closet full of clothing and the very common behavior of swapping clothes—and I created an advantage; in this case, a cash business. That summer, I always had money to go to the movies or for Slurpees at 7-Eleven.

That's all it takes: rearranging the box you have. There is incredible opportunity for innovation if you think differently about what's right in front of you to create an advantage. Where can you think differently to create an advantage in your current box?

How can you lead your team to rearrange the puzzle pieces of resources, constraints, opportunities, skill sets, and business objectives to obtain a more innovative and meaningful outcome?

As I hope you are seeing, and starting to believe, the magical key to innovation isn't in some process; it's within you.

Ignite, Scale, Sustain

When you avoid the certainty traps that silo and squelch innovation and embrace a people-first approach, you'll discover the keys to ignite, scale, and sustain innovation.

Ignite: to set on fire; to kindle. Igniting is the kickoff moment when you discover your Everyday Innovator style, when the team rallies to discover how to be high-performing, and, hence, build their competitive advantage.

Scale: to grow and progress without increased effort. When innovation spreads across everything you do and is infused into all aspects of your team's work and business, you grow. Scaling is about people across your organization thinking and acting like innovators in everything they do.

Sustain: to support, to keep up and continue with. When innovation shifts from a point-in-time exercise to a mind-set and daily action, you reach the "sustain" level, and it shows up in the DNA of your organization. You and your teams have the resources you need to bring your Everyday Innovator styles to life every single day.

This is how innovation becomes everybody's business. And, when innovation becomes everybody's business, you outmaneuver the changing marketplace and outperform the competition.

Felicia, as an Everyday Innovator, understands that the success outcomes she and her company are after begin with building the innovation skills of their people, especially the ones who often go under the radar.

"Product managers lead cross-functional teams to create, develop, and launch products. It's one of the most cross-functional disciplines. We want to build a best-in-class product management organization because we think better product management means better products means better business impact for the company."— Felicia Anderson, Collaborative Tweaker, senior director product management council and launch management at Pitney Bowes

Chapter 4

The Science of Innovation

I grew up believing I was a disorganized person. My room was always a mess, my schedule was disorganized, and I would lose my house keys multiple times a day. My family made jokes about how disheveled I was. "Oh, that's just how Tamara is," they'd say. And they were right. Ironically, as much of a hot mess as I was, I was never late. To this day, I believe that if you aren't five minutes early, you are late.

One day, while waiting in my car with nothing to do because I got to my meeting super early, I wondered how I could be a total mess *and* punctual to the max? It made me question the belief I, and everyone around me, had held for so long. It made me wonder why my desk always had stacks of papers on it and why my clothes were in heaps on the floor...yet I was never late. The two didn't seem to go together.

I decided to do a test. For one week, I would tell myself daily *I'm an organized human,* back that up with the actions of an "organized" person, and see if I could change this 40-year-old "habit." (That's right, I didn't do this until middle age.) The most amazing thing happened. This "trait" I thought was set in stone turned out to be pliable. With a mind-set shift and some focus, I could transform from a messy, disheveled person into a highly organized, neat person. Who knew?! Don't get me wrong, I have my days and still lose my keys on occasion. But the old me and the new me are drastically different.

I share this simple story with you because I want you to recognize that a lot of what we hold as "true" about ourselves is untrue or changeable.

People from across the globe come up to me after speaking, email me, and send me direct messages about how they thought they didn't have an innovative bone in their bodies, but, after taking the IQE assessment, they discovered a version of themselves that was sitting quietly inside them all along. Sometimes it just takes something as simple as an assessment or a week of testing your beliefs to realize what you held true isn't permanent and, with a mental shift and a little work, it's very flexible. There's scientific proof.

There is a lot of research and science peppered throughout this book. In this section, I want to illustrate some key foundational brain functions and neuroscience to provide a baseline to work with as you discover how you bring incredible innovation to the world. The science is important because it proves that the key to your success isn't just about willpower or motivation; the key is deep within your mind.

Old-Mind Beliefs

At one time, I believed that to be innovative you stepped outside your comfort zone and dared to be fearless (a self-proclaimed motivational speaker may have told me that). I accepted the brain was sharply divided into left and right sides: the left was all about being sequential and logical, and the right was for artsy talents like painting or dancing. Never the two sides shall meet. It followed that only a special select few had these magical innovation powers, and the rest of us were born average, with limited skills and talents. I believed that how innovative we were was set at birth. We entered this world with a fully formed, unchangeable brain. Yes, you physically grew, but the structure and capabilities of the brain were set. Like many traits we exhibit, like being disorganized or shy, it simply wasn't changeable.

But my 25 years of obsessing about how humans innovate took me down a path of working in the innovation field, qualitative research, behavioral psychology, a deep dive into neuroscience, and a study of the mechanics of the brain that blew my long-held assumptions out the door. I discovered that being innovative had nothing to do with special superpowers. In fact, it's actually an everyday skill.

As neuroscientist and Futuristic Imaginative Dr. Rex Young said to me on episode 1843 of Inside LaunchStreet podcast, "Genius is rare, creativity is common."

Intelligence versus Innovation

First, according to recent neuroscience studies, the brain structure for intelligence and creativity—or how you innovate—are different.[1] In more direct terms, "intelligence" is a well-defined pathway in the brain while "innovation" comprises loose connections across the brain. That's great news for you because it means you don't have to rely on textbook smarts or a degree after your name to be innovative.

Whether you scored high on your SATs or IQ test or, like me, have no real idea what your IQ is, you have the capacity to be innovative.

Have you ever taken two different paths to the same destination? Imagine you are meeting friends for dinner at the newly opened restaurant across town. It's past rush hour traffic, so you take the most direct route, jumping on the highway. In 20 minutes, you are there, enjoying drinks with your friends. Afterward, you rave so much about the food that your significant other wants to go there with you. This time, it's rush hour and you know the highway is going to be bumper to bumper. It's still the most direct route, but definitely not the best one to take at 5:30 p.m. on a Thursday. Instead, you decide to use side roads, weaving in and out of a bunch of little neighborhoods loosely connected by two-way roads and the little shops that line them. Along the way, you discover a new clothing store, an interesting building you somehow never noticed from the highway, and another restaurant you add to your list for date night next month. Within 40 minutes you are nibbling on appetizers and discussing some of the things you discovered by taking the side roads.

When I think about the distinction between the intelligent and the innovative mind, I'm reminded of the two routes to the restaurant. Intelligence is a highly structured superhighway. There is one way to go and there are defined barriers on either side. Innovation, on the other hand, is a bunch of loosely connected smaller roads. There are multiple roads and routes to take on any given drive, each route containing its own set of challenges, options, and discoveries.

The beauty of the human brain—and the reason I bring up this distinction—is that it contains both aspects and they're accessible to you at any given time. You use the superhighway of your brain regularly. You know what you need to do to get on the on-ramp, drive fast, and get to your destination, aka your goal. While efficient and important in many aspects, the superhighway doesn't have a lot of room for different types of thinking and outcomes. This is why it's important to get off the highway and get onto the side roads. Because you've been relying on the superhighway, the side streets may seem a little disorienting or even scary, but it's on those side roads that innovation lives, waiting for you to access it.

Whatever route you usually take to work, school, or the grocery store, I challenge you to exit and take the side roads. It's actually a great way to start priming the innovative mind. When you do "new" things or "get lost," it actually taps the problem-solving skills in your mind. You are forced to think differently about how to get from point A to point B. You can't rely on what you know or past experience, even if you sort of know the neighborhood you are driving through.

You'll see things you never noticed before, like that weird billboard with the dancing dogs. You start to figure out new ways to determine where you are and where you need to go. Instead of relying on street signs as you usually do, you might think, *Oh, the sun is setting to my left and I live east of the beach so I need to go in the other direction.* You may even hit a few dead ends—you won't go that way in the future. I think you'll find that veering over to the side streets is a no-risk yet fascinating experience.

Whole-Brain Effect

The second important neuroscientific finding shows that being innovative is not relegated to one specific portion of the brain. Researchers asked 169 people to participate in a classic creativity test while an fMRI (functioning magnetic resonance imaging) machine mapped their brain activity. They were asked to devise an alternative use for an everyday object. For example, if the object was a drinking glass, the participant might respond with a digging tool, flower vase, home for beetles.... What this study *didn't* find is as important as what it *did* find. It didn't find brain activity in one specific region. Instead, it found that the innovative mind is a whole-brain experience with a series of connections across regions.[2] This reinforces the loose connections across the mind I shared above.

The Flexible Mind

I took a welding class, partially to live out my *Flashdance* day-dreams and partially to build something with my hands. I work on a computer all day, and the idea of actually physically creating something intrigued me. In class, we started simple and worked our way into more complex structures. I ended up making a drag-onfly sculpture that sits on my desk today. It's rough and clunky, and I may be the only one who can tell it's a dragonfly, but the class was worth a few hours of my time for a week to learn a new skill. It was a fun exercise using my mind in a different way.

Have you ever, as an adult, decided to learn a new skill—knitting, glassblowing, playing guitar? Did you notice how, in doing so, you also learned new ways of thinking to master that skill? That's exactly what a group of researchers found when they asked a group of 48 participants to learn how to juggle. Why jug-gling, you might ask. Because juggling is "a complex motor skill that requires accurate bimanual arm movements, grasping, and visual tracking." In nonresearch terms, it's a cross-functional skill that requires multiple senses to complete.

In this study, they visually mapped the white matter of the brain to better understand what happens when you learn a new skill. The white matter tissue contains millions of nerve fibers, or axons, that connect and talk to each other. I envision it looking like those pictures of Earth from space at night with the lights across the cities connecting to each other in beautiful patterns. It was previously believed, like my old-mind beliefs, that the way our brains are wired is determined at birth and unchangeable.

What they discovered proves the opposite. The brain is, in fact, able to create new connections, hence new patterns of thought and skills.[3] In mapping the control group, they found changes in white matter that directly correlated to training periods. It's called neuroplasticity.

For humans, this is exciting because, if you believe you are one of those people who "don't innovate," you can learn how to acquire that skill. And when I say *acquire*, I really mean take your innovative mind off sleeper mode and put it into action.

A study out of Stanford University found that our brains have the ability to adjust and reorganize, especially in response to stim-ulus.[4] New connections can form at an amazing speed if stimu-lated through activity. With that, here's what I'd like you to do: take five minutes for yourself, grab your iPad or jump on your computer, open the YouTube app, and find a "how to" video to try out. Find something simple like calligraphy or a line dance chore-ography that doesn't require equipment. Relax, no one has to be there while you try it. The skill you choose is less important than the fact that it's new to you. This is about forming new connections in your mind, not becoming the next Instagram sensation.

Notice how your mind and body react to the new stimulus. Does it make you laugh? Are you serious and thoughtful? Do you feel empowered? Does it make you want to try other new experiences?

We built the online tool kit as a supplement to the Innovation Quotient Edge (IQE) assessment to provide innovative tools to stimulate your brain, which needs to flex and change.

Even with all the science, you still may be thinking, *They won't find any, or maybe minimal, activity in my brain...because I'm not innovative.* Untrue. You are just out of practice. What I've discovered in my work and experience is that the innovative mind is like the body. If you exercise the mind daily, it gets stronger. If you don't, it gets weak. Like the biceps or leg muscles, it needs stimulus to get stronger. Inactivity equals weakness; activity equals strength.

It doesn't matter if you think you start with a mind that barely lights up or one that blazes bright in the night sky. You are innovative.

The Lizard Brain

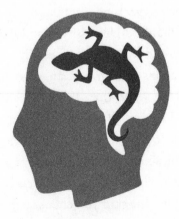

Have you ever walked down the street at night and a small shadow out of the corner of your eye makes you jump out of your shoes for seemingly no reason? Or maybe you are in a meeting and your boss responds to your idea with a tough question you weren't expecting, and your heart races and you start to sweat, making it hard for you to think of a thoughtful response. Or perhaps you really want to apply for that new position just posted in your company, so you craft an eloquent email to Human Resources singing your praises. Then, the minute it's time to hit Send, your brain says, "Nooooooo" (in slow motion), and you hit Save to Drafts instead. That's your lizard brain trying to keep you safe and comfortable.

The lizard brain is a common way of talking about the amygdala, a small and primitive part of your brain that is responsible for taking over when it senses danger.[5] In today's modern world, the danger the lizard brain is keeping you from usually isn't a saber-toothed cat waiting in the bushes to eat you, as back in the caveman days. Today, it's anything your brain perceives as risky or outside your comfort zone.

The lizard brain is your fight-or-flight mechanism. Its job is to take over instantly so that you can make decisions and take actions quickly, before the rest of your brain has time to process. In many ways the lizard brain is a gatekeeper, one that you need to get past in order to innovate.

When you innovate, the lizard brain is the chatter in the back of your brain saying "No, it's too risky" or "Don't do it, this will end badly." It wants to talk you out of innovating by telling you "You can't do this" or "Who do you think you are to even try?" It's yelling at you "THIS WILL FAIL!"

If you are walking down a dark, empty street at night, the lizard brain is your best defense against danger. But if you are trying to innovate, the lizard brain is your worst nightmare. In the section Taming the Lizard Brain (page 224), I'll dig into how to get past this necessary but frustrating gatekeeper.

For now, I just want you to know it's there. It may even be trying to shut you down as you read this book because some of the concepts are new or uncomfortable. That's okay. With your new mental framework, knowledge, and ability, we'll tame that lizard brain.

To start, let's put the lizard brain at ease by giving it the proof it needs and showing it all the styles of innovation that exist.

Chapter 5

The Style of Innovation

Be More Human

The science shows us that in the age of digital disruption and technology people simply need to be more human.

As humans, we have an innate yearning to be innovative.

"It's at the heart of what makes us human. Human creativity is what's pushed us to the pinnacle of where we find ourselves today. All animals can be intelligent, but the human animal is singularly creative and has pushed our species forward to such high pinnacles of accomplishment and challenges. Creativity allows humans to manifest their humanness."—Dr. Rex Young, neuroscientist, Imaginative Futuristic

Have you ever had the feeling of being "in the flow"? It's when you are so focused and present with what you are you doing, you lose all sense of time and surroundings. It turns out, when you are in the flow and actively and innovatively meeting the challenges in front of you, this state of being allows you to tap the reward center of your brain, releasing the feel-good chemical dopamine. Have you ever solved a particularly sticky challenge and felt a sensation of extreme accomplishment? Maybe you even patted yourself on the back? That's what happens when you innovate. The sensation of happiness and success keeps you in the flow. I want to help you create the flow every day by discovering your unique style of innovation, the force that fuels the flow.

What Is an Everyday Innovator?

Everyday Innovator: People leveraging their natural style of innovation to think differently about what's right in front of them to create an advantage.

Everyday Innovators are people like you who embrace innovation every day and across all aspects of their work and life. No special titles, no key initiatives, just you working smarter and taking a different path to success.

There is power in being an Everyday Innovator. Imagine the possibilities if you and everyone around you acted as Everyday Innovators? Think of the challenges you could solve and the opportunities you could create.

Here's the good news: you already are one. Being an Everyday Innovator isn't about changing who you are. It's about digging deep and applying what's already unique and powerful about you to the world.

Let me explain by digging into the style of innovation.

The Nine Triggers of Innovation

Being innovative is universal. We all do it. However, *how we* innovate is unique to each of us.

Much like the differences in your overall personality, you have a unique way of innovating. In fact, there are nine distinct styles of innovation. They show up in your personality, preferences, work style, behaviors, and actions. I call these styles "triggers" because they hold unique and powerful levers that unlock and initiate your innovative mind.

You can learn your style of innovation by taking the IQE assessment if you haven't already. See the Introduction to learn how. You may be able to determine what style you personify by reading the researched characteristics provided throughout this book. However, taking the IQE assessment is recommended.

As a quick introduction, the nine triggers are:

Collaborative

You create cross sections of information by tapping disparate people, experiences, and ideas.

Experiential

You think in motion, bringing ideas to life by leaping the chasm from theory to reality.

Fluid

You turn ambiguity into clarity. Uncharted territory becomes your path to new ideas.

Futuristic

You think about what's next. Tomorrow's possibilities energize you, not today's challenges.

Imaginative

Your vivid mind creates new things. You turn wild thinking into real-world ideas.

Inquisitive

Curiosity defines you. You recognize that innovation is in the questions, not the answers.

Instinctual

You tap the more intuitive part of the mind. You connect the dots in new and meaningful ways.

Risk Taker

Your adventurous spirit likes to take bold action. You willingly pursue unproven, yet high-potential, ideas.

Tweaker

You look for ways to improve and change. You reserve judgment and allow ideas time to grow.

*Understanding the nine triggers and how they come together for you personally holds the key to your ability to innovate. In fact, each person has what I call **a unique Everyday Innovator style:***

A unique combination of your top two power triggers and the presence of a dormant trigger.

Your power triggers are your natural innovation strengths, your wellspring of innovation, and your source of innovation and energy. Think of it as your brain's innate preference for creative problem solving and critical thinking.

Your dormant trigger is your least powerful. Not necessarily a weakness, but it's not your power play, and it will exhaust you if you try to innovate in that space.

What's Your Unique Everyday Innovator Style?

Will you be a Collaborative Imaginative who brings intersections of knowledge to create novel solutions? Or perhaps you are an Inquisitive Instinctual who will push past superficial assumptions to connect the dots in new and meaningful ways? Does the description for Risk Taker—always leaping into the uncomfortable—speak to you? Perhaps you read Experiential and found yourself nodding your head as you thought about the last time you felt the need to bring an idea to life.

Discovering the Everyday Innovator style that is unique to you will help you unlock your ability to:

- Perform at your peak
- Get and stay in the flow more often
- Bring more innovative ideas and solutions to your work and home life
- Apply innovation to solve your challenges, big and small
- Go after opportunities in an innovative and differentiated way
- Create breakthrough outcomes
- Have a stronger, more valued voice
- Have your voice heard by key stakeholders and decision makers

Being an Everyday Innovator is the key to making a dent in your work, your community, and the world.

If you read the Introduction, you know I have a gift for you. If you didn't read it, I suggest taking a moment and going back to understand how the code IIEB will help unlock your innovation advantage. This code is my way of bringing you the gift of innovation in a real and tangible way, in a way you can convert to action. The fact that you are reading this book tells me you are a person who strives to be high performance and high impact. The code IIEB is a gift to reward you for having that attitude toward your work and life.

One Million Innovators Challenge

Interested in participating in the One Million Innovators challenge? Read more about it in the Introduction on page 7.

PART II:
IGNITE INNOVATION

Chapter 6

Peak Performance & Adding Value

Lisa, Lowell, and Mica

Lisa was the administrative assistant to the CEO of a global consulting firm. Her forward-thinking ideas became the best practices that gave the company a competitive advantage.

—Futuristic Risk Taker

Lowell works at a retail kiosk of a major national chain. He took his conversations with customers and turned them into innovative new product ideas that have made a drastic impact on the bottom line.

—Instinctual Inquisitive

Mica runs an auditing group and his innovative leadership has transformed the team into one of the highest performing in the company.

—Fluid Imaginative

The Power of Your Everyday Innovator Style

These are the stories of Everyday Innovators like you and me. They are not the ones on the covers of magazines. They don't have sexy titles like Advocate of Happiness or Chief Experience Officer. They aren't the ones making the news or prompting a company-wide announcement even though they make a tremendous impact on an organization's ability to gain the competitive advantage and outdo the competition. Plus, they recognize that everyone has the power to innovate.

I challenge you to discover your innovation powers and have a stronger, more valued voice. Recognize that you are innovative in your own unique way. *Your* way of innovating is what's going to allow you to be an indispensable team member. View every meeting, task, or interaction as an opportunity to flex your innovation muscles.

What we've discovered through the tens of thousands of people across the globe who have taken the IQE assessment is those who own and use their ability to innovate are seen as high-performance and high-value individuals.

Be the source for the innovation energy that will seep into those around you. That's your personal competitive advantage, and you can put it to work for yourself every day.

Are you ready to have your story discovered? I hope so because you are about to unearth it.

Swimming Sideways for Innovation

When I was 10, I loved to body surf. My parents could barely get me out of the water on family beach vacations. I'd swim out with excitement, wait for the perfect wave, and then ride that bad boy in, smiling all the way. I'd stand up, laugh, and then repeat.

On one family trip in Acapulco, I was enjoying my childhood hobby when a wave of epic proportions came in. I got prepped, caught it at just the right time, and started riding it in. For a few seconds, I was loving life, in control, and showing that wave who was boss.

Within seconds, I realized I was no longer in control. I was too high on the crest, and the wave propelled me forward. I slammed into the sand as the wave crashed down on the beach. Before I could get my footing, the wave dragged me out, scraping my body along the sand. I was being pulled out to sea. The foam in my eyes prevented me from seeing which way was up. Trying not to drown, I grasped at the sand with my hands, but the ocean was too strong. Before I could say Happy Birthday, I was stuck in a riptide.

I started doing what felt natural: I doubled down. I swam harder. I kicked at double speed. I slapped my arms into the water. But no matter how hard I tried, I was swept farther out to sea.

Someone on the beach noticed me flailing. A man I'd never met but will forever be grateful to stood on the edge of the water and yelled at the top of his lungs, "Swim sideways!"

Over my panic, I heard his advice. It didn't feel natural, but what I was doing wasn't working. So I took a breath, stopped my insane swimming, turned my body, and swam to my left. Within seconds, I was out of the riptide and swimming safely to shore.

Life can be like a never-ending riptide. We swim in the hopes of reaching the shore, aka our goals, but find ourselves standing still or going backward. With our heads barely above water, we work harder and harder, not losing that feeling of being behind or overwhelmed. We do what feels natural and keep our heads down, exerting more and more effort in what we are already doing with little to no return.

But the clarity and the success we seek isn't in front of us; it's next to us. When we swim sideways, we can get out of the riptide feeling and into one of control and opportunity. It's where we find ease, clarity, and innovation in our work and home life. It's where we can breathe.

Your unique Everyday Innovator style is your ability to swim sideways in any situation, tackle any task, and work toward any goal.

Peak Performance & the Nine Triggers

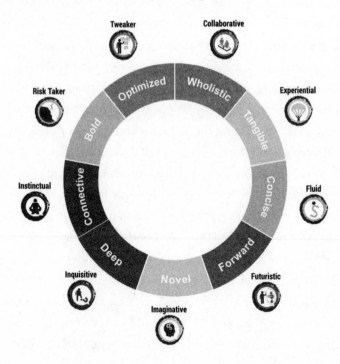

Throughout this book, I delve into the different dimensions of each trigger, including how you are motivated, language you use, how you support other triggers, how you cause friction, and managing your dormant trigger. Let's start your journey by understanding how you leverage your power triggers to be high performing, high value:

- Words that describe you
- How you perform at your peak
- How you add value

I start each trigger with a quick Everyday Innovator story. These are actually compilation stories of a range of people who embody that trigger. The stories will help you understand how and why each trigger is so powerful. In understanding that, you'll understand the value that you and those around you bring to life every single day.

I suggest that you first read what unlocks your power triggers and then read the others to better understand yourself in context of all the triggers of innovation. If you are doing this with a team, the information will give you a better understanding of how each of you innovates in relation to each other.

Collaborative

Magnetic & Inclusive

Janice has an enticing style that draws people to her work and vision. Thanks to her magnetic approach, others are eager to try new things and take risks if she is at the helm. Janice takes 20 minutes to walk down the hall to her office every day after lunch. She chats with people, runs things by them, and makes sure everyone's perspective is heard. Then, in the strategy meeting later that day, she brings strong ideas that pull together a range of perspectives.

You bring **wholistic innovation**.

You, at Your Peak:

- You have a keen ability to gather the right team and get buy-in as you drive new thinking, ensuring a higher chance of action on the back end.
- You recognize that no one person has a fully formed idea and choose to engage others as a way to inform and push your own thinking forward, creating more complete, wholistic solutions.
- Others willingly lend you their thinking and, hence, help you turn more novel ideas into fully formed opportunities.

How You Add Value:

- Collaboratives are constantly tapping into disparate people and ideas, creating random intersections where innovation thrives for yourself and others.

- You create space for many "aha" moments in a day, leading to more innovative ideas on a regular basis.
- Collaboratives like you also help the innovation process by getting others excited and motivated to drive new ideas forward.
- More of your ideas get pushed forward because you gather input and buy-in along the way.

Action-Oriented & Driven

Bill thinks in motion. He is incredibly hands-on with his work and rejects the notion that you can perfect something while it's still an idea on paper. He's often drawing up an idea to show someone, building a prototype, or talking to a client as if the solution already exists. The initiatives he moves forward with tend to be innovative and meaningful with a dash of real-world-ism to them.

You bring **tangible innovation**.

You, at Your Peak:

- You prefer real-world outcomes and experiences. Your work style puts you in constant motion and there is no idea too small or too big to put to the test of trial and error.
- The school of hard knocks is the real and only test of true viability. You may even reject or discount concepts based solely on theory or projections.
- You are often overheard saying things like "Let's see how it works before we judge" or "The real test will be when we get it out there."

How You Add Value:

- Because of your drive to bring ideas to life, you foster innovation by leaping the chasm from theory to reality.

o While many people get stuck in a state of analysis paraly-
  sis, you shift quickly to real-world action.
o While others shut down ideas before they leave paper,
  you push them forward, giving innovation a chance to
  breathe life.
- You bring a more real-world kind of innovative thinking to
  the table, giving ideas a greater chance of success in the long
  run.

Fluid

Confident & Agile

Joanna navigates constant change like it's second nature. She flows in and out of undefined situations with ease and clarity. Whether consciously or subconsciously, she seeks out situations where the process and outcomes are undefined. She finds a way to take ambiguity and confusion and turn them into clarity and innovation. It's like she plucks the brilliance out of the foggy mess.

You bring **concise innovation**.

You, at Your Peak:

- This gives you the room to flex your innovative muscles. People who thrive in ambiguity are known for being highly adaptive and accountable—a combination that allows you to proactively manage change and make rapid decisions.
- You prefer uncharted territory where you can create your own path for success instead of a highly structured environment where everything is specifically prescribed to you.
- No boundaries, no problem. Boundaries and rules actually frustrate you and hinder your ability to do your work well. When presented with too many rules, Fluids tend to rebel and step out of bounds.

How You Add Value:

- Fluids navigate the ambiguity of innovation well. What others may see as too complicated and confusing, you see as clear and purposeful.
  - o You even throw "ambiguity bombs" into a situation if you think it is becoming too predictable, forcing yourself and others outside the comfort zone.
  - o While others may shut down innovation because of its messiness, you allow chaos to thrive by accepting and moving with its natural twists and turns.
- You have the foresight and confidence to deal with the fact that where you start and where you end look nothing alike.

Futuristic

Pioneering & Visionary

Lyle is always on the leading edge of things, constantly seeking what's next. As a pioneering spirit, he seeks never-been-done ideas that will change business as it is today. He's 10 steps ahead and, hence, brilliant at innovation for what's to come versus what's already happened.

You bring **forward innovation**.

You, at Your Peak:

- While the past and present are relevant, you get energized by thinking about "Tomorrowland" and what's possible.
- You often jump ahead of your colleagues, anticipating what's next while they are still working on the current.
- You like to live in the world of possibilities and often find it a drag when people want to take your thinking to the past. Futuristics are like Magic 8 balls, seeking to answer the questions about "what will happen" and "what could be."

How You Add Value:

- As a Futuristic, you recognize that some of the most innovative ideas are based not in solving a problem of today but in creating a new behavior or opportunity for tomorrow.
  - o You push yourself and those around you to look ahead and take a longer view of the task at hand. This helps

drive ideas that are more innovative and less shortsighted and reactionary.

  o Thanks to your ability to see clearly through binoculars into the distance, you create more space for lasting innovation with impact.

- Your future-driven self means you help everyone see the forest through the trees and don't get hung up on the little things.

Imaginative

Inventive & Fresh

The less data, the better for Patricia. When the problem needs new-to-the-world ideas and solutions, she's the one who steps up to the challenge. She is recognized for her ability to ignite innovation that's going to be novel. She has a vivid mind that is always running and creating new things. She is a dreamer with the ability to turn wild thinking into real-world ideas.

You bring **novel innovation**.

You, at Your Peak:

- Your mind goes beyond the facts at hand and pulls from the unknown.
- The idea of doing what's always been done bothers you when there is so much new space to explore. Novel ideas and creative approaches are always percolating in your mind.
- Imaginatives push the boundaries of possibilities by redefining the borders of reality to fit their ideas.

How You Add Value:

- Imaginatives are key to innovation because you add much-needed magical thinking to your work. Your thinking is imaginative, purposeful, and novel—the perfect recipe for innovation.

o Furthermore, when others are banging their heads against the wall, you tap your imagination for innovative approaches that take you around, over, and through the wall.

o It requires a lot of imagination to deal with an ever-changing world, where there is no precedence for what we are dealing with. Your imagination tackles the fast-paced world with ease, helping you and your team overcome challenges.

- Imaginatives push the boundaries of possibilities by redefining the borders of reality to fit their ideas.

Inquisitive

Intense & Curious

Ari always has questions. Even when everyone else is done with the meeting and decisions have been made, Ari has 10 more questions for his team. While the rest of us may take things at a superficial level, Ari digs and challenges assumptions and decisions. Ari is known for uncovering innovation the rest of us miss.

You bring **deep innovation**.

You, at Your Peak:

- In your mind, every answer leads to 10 more questions. You love being able to ask as many questions as you possibly can.
- Your curious nature challenges the way things are done, often bending the rules when it's advantageous to you.
- While Inquisitives take in a lot of information, you make decisions based on how you perceive the combination of the facts versus on one or two facts alone.

How You Add Value:

- Inquisitive people are great for unraveling daunting problems and opportunities, making the complex simple.
  - Because you are always asking "Why" and "How," you have a tendency to initiate new perspectives and thinking.

Not taking things at face value helps you generate innovative ideas.

o You aren't afraid to challenge groupthink and ask the questions others are afraid to ask.

- Innovation is often found in the questions, not the answers, and you spend a lot of time asking questions.

Instinctual

Insightful & Swift

Vin speaks from the gut, sometimes unable to explain why he has the idea or how he knows something to be true. He brings incredible insights to the team because he is able to see patterns and trends before others. His team knows to go to him if they want the big picture or need to understand how things fit together. His innovative ideas are insightful and robust.

You bring **connective innovation**.

You, at Your Peak:

- You often "sense" or "feel" ideas before you can rationally explain them.
- Instinctuals have an inner compass that guides their thinking. While this compass may seem unexplainable to others, it is simply a matter of your ability to pull together a wide range of facts, experiences, and knowledge.
- Your ideas and opinions are formed by a larger, more circuitous pattern of thought, making them naturally more creative.

How You Add Value:

- Because of the Instinctual's ability to connect a lot of dots and your sixth sense for what will happen next, you are great at exploring new patterns of thinking.

o You push innovation by helping yourself and others connect the dots in new and meaningful ways.

o You tend to be decisive because you are comfortable making gut decisions and don't feel the need to wait for all the facts to come in. In innovation, this can be the difference between moving forward and being dead in the water.

- Your quick insight ensures that innovation is always present no matter what you are doing.

Risk Taker

Audacious & Fearless

Giana has an adventurous spirit and is willing to take bold actions. When called upon to do something uncomfortable, she is the first to jump in. She has a high tolerance for risk and even seeks out seemingly intimidating situations. Her team recognizes her as the one to tackle the big ideas and moves because she will leap and figure it out as she goes. Giana is always willing to play in those uncomfortable spaces, so her innovation is bold and tends to push boundaries.

You bring **bold innovation**.

You, at Your Peak:

- Because of your willingness to put yourself out there, you often seek out new people and experiences.
- The thrill of taking the risk is as invigorating as the success it could produce.
- To Risk Takers, every moment is an opportunity to reach for higher goals.

How You Add Value:

- You push the innovation process forward and get people out of the box where innovation dies.
  - While others get stuck or paralyzed at parts of the journey that require bold decisions and actions, you move quickly into them.

o Your fearless nature means you are willing to take more leaps of faith and pursue unproven yet high-potential work.

■ Your willingness to take smart risks means you are more likely to pursue bolder, more innovative ideas that have the potential for greater impact.

Tweaker

Transformative & Dynamic

For Mitch, being in flux is a state he actually prefers. To him, things aren't final, they're just ready for improvement. He is the one asking what did and didn't work at every stage of a project. Mitch knows that one little adjustment could make all the difference, so he doesn't give up. His tiny shifts, edits, and tweaks uncover innovation with massive impact. His leaders know he's the one to take a project or idea and optimize it when others hit the wall.

You bring **optimized innovation**.

You, at Your Peak:

- For you, there is no such thing as failure or success, especially during the early stages of a project. It's more about outcomes that help you determine what to do next.
- You reject the concept of striving for perfection (which kills innovation) and instead focus on making progress.
- You put your ideas out there early and then tweak until you get them right. You know that hitting the big win could be one tweak away from where you are right now.

How You Add Value:

- People who constantly tweak avoid judging ideas as failures or successes too early, which is critical for innovation.

Instead, Tweakers focus on incremental yet important improvements at every step of the way.

- o You keep innovation alive by finding small yet important opportunities to continually improve.
- o In many ways you are the gardener of innovation, planting idea seeds and then giving them the nourishment and time to grow into fully formed idea plants.
- While others quit easily and early, you stick it out and tend to get those big wins because of it.

How Do You Compare?

Now that you've discovered your Everyday Innovator style, I bet you are wondering how you compare to the rest of the world. Take a look at the pie chart below, which is a compilation of the tens of thousands of people who have taken the IQE across the globe.

My hope is you take two things away from this pie chart. First, if you look at the percentages, I hope you see how unique you really are. Poppy, who is an Inquisitive Instinctual, shares her style with 31 percent of people around the world; Oliver, who is a Fluid Futuristic, with only 16 percent of people. Second, while how you innovate is unique to you, I hope this also reinforces that being innovative is common. It's across cultures, ages, races, genders, levels of experience, industries, etc.

How you compare on this chart is also how you stand out.

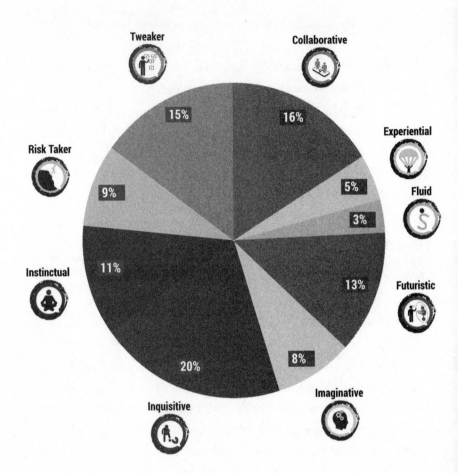

Chapter 7

Apply Your Everyday Innovator Superpowers

Kelly, the Collaborative Tweaker

To further define the Everyday Innovator talents you have, we pull the top two power triggers in your profile. The magic happens at the intersection of your two power triggers. For Kelly, that occurs at the intersection of Collaborative and Tweaker.

Kelly works for the Army Research Labs (ARL), a large government agency with plenty of hierarchy. Their work is vital for keeping our military safe and competitive on the battlefield. Kelly isn't one of the supercool researchers who spend their days experimenting in the labs with robots, chemicals, and things behind closed doors they can't show a civilian like me. She is in operations—specifically, the administrative staff. Her job, like that of her counterparts, is to ensure that big initiatives and the day-to-day operations of the organization run smoothly. Kelly is incredible at her job.

Like many organizations, ARL suffers from siloed and specialized innovation. Those who experiment are the "mad" innovative geniuses, and those who run operations and projects aren't.

They are seen as the doers of tasks. However, this organization has visionary leadership, and Kelly is trying to improve herself and those around her.

ARL leadership recognizes how important it is to instill innovative mind-sets in all their employees. They brought me in to deploy the Innovation Quotient Edge (IQE) and talk about innovation with the team. Imagine how intimidating it is to stand in front of an auditorium full of operations specialists, researchers, and generals in fatigues. However, whenever I start doing some of my interactive audience exercises, individuals loosen up with smiles and laughter.

When we tackle the identification of innovation triggers, Kelly discovers she is a Collaborative Tweaker. Her natural innovative strengths revolve around connection and optimization. If you have the honor of meeting Kelly, you'll discover she exudes her Everyday Innovator style. As an incredible communicator, she finds reasons to reach out to people. She is known for her ability to take something that is stalled and find that one little adjustment to put it back on track.

When she realized her superpowers far exceeded how she acted day to day, she immediately took action. She set up what she called *cohorts* where she and her once-siloed colleagues connect monthly to share best practices, challenges, and resources. This did two things. First, it broke down walls. Prior to cohorts, her colleagues were cloistered in their teams, doing their work without a dotted line or a process that connected them on a continual basis. Second, creating cohorts fed Kelly's need to be at a cross section of input, collecting thoughts, perspectives, and ideas. She fuels her innovation fires in these meetings.

Thanks in part to our work together, Kelly's innovative ideas flow, and she elevates the work of those around her. Kelly is the master at taking something that's been started and elevating it to an entirely new level. When ARL started exploring the idea of a podcast, Kelly reached out to me to better understand the ins and outs of creating a podcast. She brought that knowledge back to her leaders, using her network to gain an advantage and go further faster. She's a big reason ARL now has an incredible podcast any of us can enjoy on iTunes.

Kelly is an Everyday Innovator dedicated to making a big impact in the work she faces every day and leading others to do the same. Her peers and her bosses continually recognize her for her innovative and proactive approach to her work.

As the iconic Dolly Parton once said, "Find out who you are and do it on purpose." Kelly does just that. Now, it's your turn.

Tapping your innovative mind will help you bring your A game and work in the flow more often and more easily. It won't be exhausting. In fact, it will be energizing. There are daily opportunities to put your Everyday Innovator into action to gain the advantage if you are open to them. Here are a few:

#1: Tackle Your Biggest Challenges

In today's fast-paced world, you are required to deal with the challenges that have been rearing their ugly heads for months, maybe even years, plus you need to solve new-to-the-world challenges. As the world changes, so do the challenges you face.

Fortunately, you are an Everyday Innovator, meaning you have the skills needed to tackle anything that comes your way, big or small. Challenges like:

- How will you solve the declining sales of your brand?
- What will you do to compete against the new competitor trying to disrupt the category?

- What will it take to overcome the bottleneck that affects your ability to perform well?
- How will you get buy-in from that guy on your team who tends to shut everything down?
- How are you going to add value when your company just installed a new technology that does part of your job?
- How are you going to squeeze in all the meetings on your calendar today when half your day is double-booked?
- How are you going to juggle your shifting priorities at work and home?

What are the challenges you are tackling? Take a second to write them down. As you redevelop your ability to innovate, you'll discover a new lens through which to view those challenges and, more important, an innovative approach to solving them.

You will see how not only to get over the wall, but you will discover ways to go around, through, and under the wall—and maybe remove the wall completely. This puts you in a position of tremendous competitive advantage if you can create meaningful and innovative solutions. Bringing that type of thinking to your work will set you apart fast. Those you seek to impress will notice your performance and results. And you'll go to bed at night with a tremendous amount of satisfaction in how you tackled your day.

Jess worked at a window-blind company as a sales rep. The company had been around since long before she was born, and Jess appreciated the tried-and-true processes she was able to plug into. But after a few months of sales calls, she noticed that every time they processed a new customer order there was a glitch that slowed down the process. The slowdown wasn't necessarily noticeable to the customer, but it did create confusion and extra work internally. The order forms were missing spaces for a few key pieces of information that helped her do her job and let the warehouse know they were pulling the right blinds.

One day, she went to talk to the warehouse guys and found herself in a line with four other sales reps needing to have the same conversation. Jerry, who was standing in front of her, had been with the company since the beginning, so she asked him why they did this one piece of information this way. He shrugged and said, "It's the way we've always done it."

Well, that's not good enough, thought Jess.

Jess is an Inquisitive Risk Taker, which means she innovates by steeping herself in inquiry and then gets uncomfortable and takes the leap as she figures it out. That day, Jess asked people across the organization about this issue: Why do we do it this way? How did this process begin? Did we always need this information? Who is responsible for the system? How helpful would it be in the warehouse to know this about the customer? After lots of questions to others and herself, Jess leapt into action. She knew she couldn't get approval to do an overhaul of their sales system—that would require a massive investment of time, money, and technology. That could be her end goal, but she first needed to find a small, short-term solution to get them partway there.

She created an order amendment form that had all the customer information and the missing piece of information in two ways. First, it had a space for her to write it the way a salesperson would need the information; a second section had check boxes for how that information would translate into the product style and size. Everyone had the information they needed. Then she placed a clipboard and a box in the warehouse where the team gathered to print out the day's orders. The clipboard contained the blank forms for the salespeople to fill out; the box was for the completed forms. She then went to each group and gave them instructions on the new process. At first, people were resistant. They were, after all, set in their ways. But every time she saw Jerry or anyone else walk into the warehouse to have that conversation, she kindly directed them to the new process. Over time, the alternative paperwork was accepted, and Jess was happy. She saved herself an hour a day with this new process, and she suspected it was about the same for the others. With eight people on the sales staff and six in the warehouse, that totaled 14 hours a week reclaimed to be applied to doing their jobs—a day and a half of previously wasted time. Jess was elated.

After a month, the president and founder of the company noticed the lack of busy chatter in the warehouse; orders were going out faster; and he was surprised by the increase in sales in a month that was usually flat. At the next company-wide picnic, the president of the company made two announcements: First, he recognized Jess with lots of accolades and a promotion. She may not have been at the company the longest, but her impact was felt everywhere. Second, he announced the company was going to invest in new technology that would streamline the process for everyone. The clipboard solution worked so well he recognized the need to go a few steps further. This happened because Jess, the Inquisitive Risk Taker, applied her innovation superpowers to a challenge everyone else had accepted as part of the process.

In the following chart, you'll find very simple exercises that each power trigger can do to activate and supercharge your innovation skills. This is how you come up with solutions as Jess did. Use the two that correlate to your Everyday Innovator style.

If you are an Imaginative Inquisitive, you might want to walk away from your desk for five minutes, think about something else, and then come back and develop three more questions. If you are an Experiential Collaborative, you might want to sketch out your thinking on a piece of paper and then try to solve your challenge as if you were a different stakeholder (if you are in sales, think from the customer perspective). Do this and the innovation will flow.

Here's a hint for better teamwork. To tap the power of the Everyday Innovators on your team, bring the exercises that speak to them to your next meeting. If you have a Collaborative Instinctual, bring an exercise around smashing random (see the Power Trigger chart for more details) and ask them how they feel about an idea. If you have a Fluid Tweaker, ask them to clarify a messy situation and then do an exercise involving tweaking ideas that have been formed.

Power Trigger	Exercises		
Collaborative	Collect others' thinking	Cross over and connect random things from your life and work	Look at the challenge as if you were someone else with a different perspective
Experiential	Make a rough prototype of the challenge to innovate against	Sketch it out in a drawing and ask someone else to give you input	Test an idea with one person and build from that conversation
Fluid	Throw an ambiguity bomb	Focus on the less defined elements	Pull out the clear and concise nuggets
Futuristic	Ask "How could we...?" three times, in three different ways	Think about the challenge from 10 steps ahead and work backward from there	Apply "What if..." thinking. Make your what-ifs small at first and then totally wild and bold
Imaginative	Remove some information, then figure out how to solve an issue	Walk away from your work for five minutes to do something drastically different, and then come back to it	Ask "Where's the new in this?" or "How can I add new to this?"

Power Trigger	Exercises		
Inquisitive	Ask "What if this weren't the solution we went with?"	Dig deeper by asking three more questions even if you think you know the answer	Find the problem to the problem, then find the problem that caused that problem, then solve
Instinctual	Speak your ideas fast and without judgment, then work backward into rationalizing them	Collect a range of random dots to connect with your challenge and search for the patterns and insights	Start your thoughts with "I feel" to tap your intuitive side
Risk Taker	Don't analyze, just leap into action and figure it out as you go	Take a small risk like disagreeing, trying something new, playing devil's advocate	Share an uncomfortable or crazy idea with someone
Tweaker	Find one adjustment to the idea you are working on	Look at the idea from a slightly different perspective; from the view of someone up- or downstream from you	Ask someone else to talk first, then build on their thinking

#2: Discover Your Greatest Opportunities

"Your diamonds are not in far distant mountains or in yonder seas; they are in your own backyard, if you but dig for them.

—Russell H. Conwell

Your day isn't filled with challenges only; it's also filled with incredible opportunities. Most of them are staring you in the face. You haven't seen them because you haven't been looking through an innovative lens. Being an Everyday Innovator will motivate you to bring innovation into the world, and it will give you the ability to see the innovation around you.

Swiss engineer George de Mestral was an avid hunter, always taking his dog with him. On one particular trip, he took note of the thistles that stuck to his socks and his dog. His curiosity impelled him to look at the annoying plant under a microscope. He discovered that little burdock burr had hooks that made it stick to almost any fabric or fur, anything with loops.[1] Guess what being curious and looking through an innovative lens on that fateful hunting trip led to: the creation of Velcro, a practical solution for fastening many products, like clothing, pockets, and bags.

The story goes that Dr. Alexander Fleming ran a sloppy lab. But that sloppiness presented an opportunity for innovation that changed the world. Dr. Fleming accidently left out cultures of Staphylococcus aureus and, upon returning from a two-week trip, he discovered their growth had been prevented by a mold called Penicillium notatum.[2] That's right! Modern antibiotics came from an accident and one man's ability to see the opportunity in that accident.

My favorite story behind innovation is the invention of the Slinky. As an engineer in the US Navy, Richard James was trying to find a way to keep the sensitive instruments he used on the ship from rocking themselves to breaking points. He knocked one of his prototypes on the floor and, instead of breaking or rolling, it "slinked" away.[3] In that moment, the child's toy many of you played with and probably still enjoy was created because Richard didn't shrug it off; he saw the opportunity in the mistake.

Keep that innovation lens on, and I promise you'll see more opportunities and innovation than you ever thought possible.

#3: Have a Stronger, More Valued Voice

Whether you face customers, reside in the deep internal workings of your organization, head the company, work in the field, or are a business owner, your ability to provide massive value to the marketplace is essential for survival. Being a high performer isn't about doing your job, it's about the added value you bring to the table. What's on your job description is just the cost of entry these days. What really helps you stand out and succeed is the intangible: the strategic thinking, the collaboration, the innovation, the differentiated value.

Remember, your organization, regardless if it's in healthcare, manufacturing, consumer goods, business-to-business services, government, nonprofit, etc., is experiencing massive change. None of us is immune to change's impact, so leadership is leaning on you and, hopefully, everyone in the organization to drive innovation. As an Everyday Innovator, this is your greatest value and competitive advantage. You have the opportunity to be that voice and doer of innovation.

Think about how your Everyday Innovator style can contribute at this level more often because, when you realize your innovation potential, it's not only possible, it's essential. Here's how each power trigger adds value in a way that is sought and recognized by those around you. Look for the two that make up your power triggers and then read how others around you provide value in their best way possible. Then intentionally put it into action.

Power Trigger	How You Add Value:
Collaborative	Pull people together; get buy-in; see from lots of perspectives, which means you also see the strengths and the weaknesses of ideas before others. Show your colleagues, leaders, clients.
Experiential	Create momentum when things stall; show colleagues, leaders, clients how their ideas play out in the real world; this creates innovation that works because you come from a "test it" mind-set. Share your test and results so your colleagues and bosses see it, too.
Fluid	Help people see the clarity and opportunity in a messy situation; in the confusion, find the innovation for people.
Futuristic	Show your colleagues, leaders, and clients the impact of their work; deliver ideas that don't provide a solution for today only but move them into the future.
Imaginative	Help those around you find imaginative solutions for a new and changing marketplace.
Inquisitive	Ask thought-provoking questions that make everyone around you think differently.
Instinctual	Bring the patterns and the insights that others don't see to your colleagues and clients. Help them understand how those patterns impact them.
Risk Taker	Get your colleagues and clients out of analysis paralysis; show them the big picture; make their thinking even bigger and bolder.
Tweaker	Find the high-impact adjustments that un-stall projects; optimize and set up for greater success what your colleagues and clients build.

Imagine how people will perk up and listen if you bring this type of thinking and ideas every time they interact with you. Think about how your boss or client will react when they realize you are helping them succeed.

How will your colleagues perceive you when you perform at your peak, not only when you do the work you love, but in all your actions? Providing this type of innovative thinking and skill to your colleagues, leaders, and even clients makes you the one with the stronger, more valued voice. Your voice is sought after and listened to when you bring innovation to the table.

#4: Create Breakthrough Outcomes

Brian Benstock is a down-to-earth kind of guy. In fact, if he introduces himself to you at a party, he won't tell you he's a vice president or a general manager, he'll tell you point-blank that he sells Hondas. Brian has been in the car industry since 1982 and, as he shared with me, "I'm in an industry that is holding on for dear life and fighting change every step of the way. Not in technology and AI (artificial intelligence), but in how the car dealership business operates." If you think about the old-school car dealership and car commercials, you see his point. But as an Inquisitive Tweaker, Brian questioned how business was being conducted and found inspiration for improvement in the change all around him. Uber came on the scene and gave customers shared control. Amazon allowed customers to compare and shop for just about anything. All of this is in direct conflict with the traditional dealership floor he was managing. Like many in legacy industries, Brian was doing what he'd always done. As he shared with me, "We were spending upwards of $100,000 a month for print advertising that we couldn't even prove was doing anything... because we always had."

Brian took a portion of that traditional spending and applied it toward digital marketing, which at the time was still the Wild West of unproven territory. Then he took it a step further by placing a "buy button" on his website. His colleagues scoffed at him, "No one will buy a car online." They were wrong.

Eventually, Brian tackled the dealership itself. He thought, *What are our customers' real frustrations?* It isn't buying a car, it's servicing that car. Most of us have experienced the inconvenient appointments, the bad coffee, and the time wasted watching judge shows on the small, somewhat staticky TV in the corner. This is where Brian and his team went big and bold. He tied Google voice to their service department so his customers could easily reach them online. Then (and here's where I think it gets really innovative), instead of having to carve out my day to twiddle my thumbs at the dealership, his team schedules a time to pick up the car at your house (or work) and deliver it back when it's ready.

When you apply your Everyday Innovator style daily, you create breakthrough results. It doesn't happen by looking in the same box, at the same information, in the same way. It happens by rearranging the box you have. It happens through your ability to think differently about what's right in front of you (as the definition of innovation states). That's what Brian did for his business to become a top dealership and innovator.

#5: Spread Innovation Far and Wide

Karl and I were sitting in a café on Saturday morning, drinking coffee and having a fairly serious conversation about life. The café was packed with people, but we did a pretty good job of ignoring them. The line for coffee zigzagged through the café. I heard a few people in line laughing but didn't think much of it. A few more people started laughing. Then a few more…and a few more. Before I knew it, the tables next to us were smiling broadly and laughing heartily. The entire café was laughing hysterically. Karl and I looked around in confusion. I tried to catch his eye to ask him what the heck was going on, but he too started laughing.

"What are you laughing at?" I asked.

He said, "I don't know but I can't help myself."

And neither could I. Before I knew it, I was laughing and I had no idea why.

Eventually it died down and I noticed the four people standing in line high-fiving each other. I asked them what that was all about. One of them said, "Oh, it's a laugh mob. Kind of like a dance mob but with laughing."

"What's the point?" I asked.

"To get everyone laughing. No one can resist," he responded.

He was right. Laughing is contagious, and that day in the café proved it. Three people turned into 10, which turned into 20 and, eventually, 50-ish people were laughing their behinds off for no apparent reason.

Laughter is highly contagious and so is innovation. When you open the doors of innovation, those around you, especially those who have been waiting for permission to innovate, will eagerly follow your lead. Of course, you'll have your resisters and you'll bump up against their legacy thinking along the way, but the truth is more people than not want to be innovative. It's human nature to want to think critically and solve problems in innovative ways. An innovative attitude will give you the tailwind you need to get even the most stodgy, crusty naysayer to open up, at least a little. Overall, you'll discover that your innovative energy will ripple out to those around you.

Like the guy in the café who laughed first, don't be afraid to be the first one to unlock innovation. Others will join you. You can be the epicenter of an innovation movement if you choose to be.

At this point, I hope you're thinking, *Holy Batman! I am powerful!* Excuse the boldness, but you are. I see it over and over in my work. The light in the eyes of newly liberated innovators begins to shine brighter as they recognize the incredible purpose and value they bring to the world, to their communities, work, and families. However, the key to that power is commitment and action. Without that, you are just nodding your head and going back to business as usual. You need to commit to being an Everyday Innovator. You need to own the fact that innovation is everybody's business, most importantly yours.

Everyday Innovator User Manuals

You have a user manual for your new dishwasher, your car, your computer, the technology you use, the processes you follow to do your job.... The only thing missing is a user's guide for the most important piece of the puzzle—you. It's easy to assume people automatically know how you work best, what motivates you, and how to best leverage you. This is especially true when it comes to how you innovate and contribute. However, it's like expecting your partner to read your mind when you want a certain mode of behavior from them.

Jennifer Wade, the 2019 president of the Meetings Industry Council board, recognizes the importance of understanding and continuing to make front and center how individuals tick. The board is comprised of a diverse set of people from various subsets of the meetings-and-events industry coming together to lead in an industry that regularly faces massive change. She knows that if she is going to build strong camaraderie and ignite innovation and collaboration under a shared purpose, they are going to have to learn how to work together before tackling their challenges and opportunities. With this in mind, Jennifer has her board dig deep into their Everyday Innovator styles during their big strategy retreat, where they come together to kick off the year. When the lightbulbs go on, and the group has some honest and revelatory conversations about how they each add value and can come together as a team, the group agrees it is important to keep their newfound information about themselves front and center. They don't want to forget how to be their best and bring out the best in everyone else around the table. Indeed, each of their table name tags has not only their name but also their unique Everyday Innovator styles.

Likewise, why not let people know how to engage with you? Imagine how progressive the interaction will be when someone walks into your office and sees your Risk Taker Tweaker icons on your desk. Conversely, how much more powerful would your next meeting be if the Everyday Innovator's User Manuals were front and center around the room? If nothing else, you'd be reminded to tap the power of the diversity in the room; that alone will elevate the outcome.

"Having our Everyday Innovator styles front and center has not only kept the innovation momentum going, but also allowed each of us to recognize and leverage each other for the uniqueness we bring. Our User Manual postcards remind us daily how to perform at our peaks and bring that out in others. We are a stronger team because of it."

—Jennifer Wade, MIC 2019 president,
Tweaker Collaborative

Your user manual is your personal guide to how you operate best. It doesn't hurt to be reminded about your own unique operations. I think we often forget how we work best even though we live in our bodies every day. Engaging with someone else, it's beneficial to remind them of or introduce them to your Everyday Innovator style. When I speak to groups, I often bring postcards that include their Everyday Innovator style on the front and a quick user's guide on the back. Hands down, it's audiences' favorite takeaway.

Here are two powerful tools to act as reminders of your strengths:

#1 Take a Picture: On the following pages you will find the icons and a quick user manual for each of the thirty-six Everyday Innovator style combinations. Find yours, take a picture, print it, and place it somewhere you'll see daily.

#2 Get Your User Manual: On the shop at our website, you will find a User Manual Toolkit for each of the styles of innovation. Get yours. It will include your colorful postcard and much more.

I highly suggest you find some way to put your user manual front and center where you and those around you will see it daily.

The user manuals for each of the 36 Everyday Innovator styles are listed here in alphabetical order. *Note: If your report shows Imaginative Risk Taker, it's the same as the card that might have Risk Taker listed first.* The order of your two power triggers isn't important. What is important is that those two triggers combine to be your power play.

Everyday Innovator User Manual: Collaborative + Fluid

Collaborative   Fluid

Magnetic—Inclusive—Confident—Agile

I speak with inclusive and movement-based language that includes the words *we, together, collectively, navigate, flow,* and *try out.*

Leverage me when you feel like your thinking is missing alternate perspectives or have a particularly messy and unclear challenge that needs clarity.

I'm motivated by building connections between people and ideas and creating clarity in situations and ideas.

Collaborative + Futuristic

Collaborative   Futuristic

Magnetic—Inclusive—Pioneering—Visionary

I speak with inclusive and forward-motion language that includes the words *we, together, collectively, build, next steps,* and *envision.*

Leverage me when you feel like your thinking is missing alternate perspectives or have a challenge that requires insight around how today's work will impact tomorrow's outcomes.

I'm motivated by building connections between people and ideas and creating new paths to the future.

Collaborative + Imaginative

Magnetic—Inclusive—Inventive—Fresh

I speak with inclusive and possibility language that includes the words *we, together, collectively, what about, imagine,* and *create.*

Leverage me when you feel like your thinking is missing alternate perspectives or have a challenge that needs an infusion of fresh thinking.

I'm motivated by building connections between people and ideas and creating novel ideas.

Collaborative + Inquisitive

Magnetic—Inclusive—Intense—Curious

I speak with inclusive and clarifying language that includes the words *we, together, collectively, how, why, what if,* and *how come.*

Leverage me when you feel like your thinking is missing alternate perspectives or have a challenge that needs some assumption busting and digging to find the innovation.

I'm motivated by building connections between people and ideas and uncovering challenges and solutions.

Collaborative + Instinctual

Collaborative   Instinctual

Magnetic—Inclusive—Insightful—Swift

I speak with inclusive and heart-based language that includes the words *we, together, collectively, I feel, I wonder,* and *believe.*

Leverage me when you feel like your thinking is missing alternate perspectives or have a challenge where current thinking feels too myopic and disconnected.

I'm motivated by building links between people and feeling connected to people and work.

Collaborative + Tweaker

Collaborative   Tweaker

Magnetic—Inclusive—Focused—Dynamic

I speak with inclusive and questioning language that includes the words *we, together, collectively, what's working, evolve,* and *edit.*

Leverage me when you feel like your thinking is missing alternate perspectives or have a challenge where others have given up, but you know there's something there worth pursuing.

I'm motivated by building connections between people and ideas and finding the gaps and solutions.

Collaborative + Experiential

Collaborative Experiential

Magnetic—Inclusive—Action Oriented—Driven

I speak with inclusive and reality-based language that includes the words *we, together, collectively, testing it out, real world,* and *experiment.*

Leverage me when you feel like your thinking is missing alternate perspectives or have a challenge or idea that has stalled and needs forward motion.

I'm motivated by creating connections between people and ideas, building new ideas, and taking action.

Fluid + Inquisitive

Fluid Inquisitive

Confident—Agile—Intense—Curious

I speak with movement-based and clarifying language that includes the words *navigate, flow, try out, how, why, what if,* and *how about.*

Leverage me when your thinking feels messy and unclear or you have a challenge that needs some assumption busting and digging to find the innovation.

I'm motivated by creating clarity in situations and ideas and uncovering challenges and solutions.

Fluid + Instinctual

Confident—Agile—Insightful—Swift

I speak with movement-based and heart-based language that includes the words *navigate, flow, try out, I feel, I wonder,* and *I believe.*

Leverage me when your thinking feels messy and unclear or you have a challenge where current thinking feels too myopic and disconnected.

I'm motivated by creating clarity in situations and ideas and feeling connected to my work and people.

Fluid + Experiential

Confident—Agile—Action Oriented—Driven

I speak with movement-based and reality-based language that includes the words *navigate, flow, try out, test it out, real world,* and *experiment.*

Leverage me when your thinking feels messy and unclear or you have a challenge or idea that has stalled and needs forward motion.

I'm motivated by creating clarity in situations and ideas, building ideas, and taking action.

Fluid + Tweaker

Fluid   Tweaker

Confident—Agile—Focused—Dynamic

I speak with movement-based and questioning language that includes the words *navigate, flow, try out, what's working, evolve, edit,* and *modify.*

Leverage me when your thinking feels messy and unclear or you have a challenge where others have given up but you know there's something there worth pursuing.

I'm motivated by creating clarity in situations and ideas and finding the gaps and solutions.

Futuristic + Experiential

Futuristic   Experiential

Pioneering—Visionary—Real World—Driven

I speak with possibility and reality-based language that includes the words *build, next steps, envision, test it out, real world,* and *experiment.*

Leverage me when your thinking is stuck in the past or you have a challenge or idea that has stalled and needs forward motion.

I'm motivated by building ideas and paths to the future, building ideas, and taking action.

Futuristic + Fluid

Futuristic   Fluid

Pioneering—Visionary—Agile—Confident

I speak with forward-motion and movement-based language that includes the words *build, envision, navigate, flow,* and *try out.*

Leverage me when your thinking is stuck in the past or you have a particularly messy and unclear challenge that needs clarity.

I'm motivated by building ideas and paths to the future and creating clarity in situations and ideas.

Futuristic + Inquisitive

Futuristic   Inquisitive

Pioneering—Visionary—Insightful—Swift

I speak with possibility and clarifying language that includes the words *build, next steps, envision, how, why, what about,* and *what if.*

Leverage me when your thinking is stuck in the past or you have a challenge that needs some assumption busting and digging to find the innovation.

I'm motivated by building ideas and paths to the future and uncovering challenges and solutions.

Futuristic + Instinctual

Futuristic   Instinctual

Pioneering—Visionary—Insightful—Swift

I speak with forward-motion and heart-based language that includes the words *build, next steps, envision, I feel, I wonder,* and *believe.*

Leverage me when your thinking is stuck in the past or you have a challenge where current thinking feels too myopic and disconnected.

I'm motivated by building ideas and paths to the future and feeling connected to my work and people.

Futuristic + Tweaker

Futuristic   Tweaker

Pioneering—Visionary—Focused—Dynamic

I speak with possibility and questioning language that includes the words *build, next steps, envision, what's working, evolve, edit,* and *modify.*

Leverage me when your thinking is stuck in the past or you have a challenge where others have given up but you know there's something there worth pursuing.

I'm motivated by building ideas and paths to the future and finding the gaps and solutions.

Imaginative + Experiential

Inventive—Fresh—Action Oriented—Driven

I speak with possibility and reality-based language that includes the words *how about, imagine, create, testing it out, real world,* and *experiment.*

Leverage me when you feel overwhelmed by the facts and can't find the innovation or have a challenge or idea that has stalled and needs forward motion.

I'm motivated by creating novel ideas, building on them, and taking action.

Imaginative + Fluid

Inventive—Fresh—Agile—Confident

I speak with possibility and movement-based language that includes the words *how about, imagine, create, navigate, flow,* and *try out.*

Leverage me when you feel overwhelmed by the facts and can't find the innovation or have a particularly messy and unclear challenge that needs clarity.

I'm motivated by building novel ideas and creating clarity in situations and ideas.

Imaginative + Futuristic

Imaginative   Futuristic

Inventive—Fresh—Pioneering—Visionary

I speak with possibility and forward-motion language that includes the words *how about, imagine, build, next steps,* and *envision.*

Leverage me when you feel overwhelmed by the facts and can't find the innovation or have a challenge that requires insight around how today's work will impact tomorrow's outcomes.

I'm motivated by creating novel directions and building paths to the future.

Imaginative + Inquisitive

Imaginative   Inquisitive

Inventive—Fresh—Intense—Curious

I speak with possibility and clarifying language that includes the words *how about, imagine, create, how, why, what about,* and *what if.*

Leverage me when you feel overwhelmed by the facts and can't find the innovation or have a challenge that needs some assumption busting and digging to find the innovation.

I'm motivated by building novel ideas and uncovering challenges and solutions.

Imaginative + Instinctual

Inventive—Fresh—Insightful—Swift

I speak with possibility and heart-based language that includes the words *how about, imagine, create, I feel, I wonder* and *believe.*

Leverage me when you feel overwhelmed by the facts and can't find the innovation or have a challenge where current thinking feels too myopic and disconnected.

I'm motivated by building novel ideas and feeling connected to people and work.

Imaginative + Tweaker

Inventive—Fresh—Focused—Dynamic

I speak with possibility and questioning language that includes the words *how about, imagine, create, what's working, evolve, edit,* and *change.*

Leverage me when you feel overwhelmed by the facts and can't find the innovation or have a challenge where others have given up but you know there's something there worth pursuing.

I'm motivated by building novel ideas and finding the gaps and solutions.

Inquisitive + Experiential

Intense—Curious—Action Oriented—Driven

I speak with questioning and reality-based language that includes the words *how, why, what about, test it out, real world,* and *experiment.*

Leverage me when you are stuck down one path and need help seeing things differently or have a challenge or idea that has stalled and needs forward motion.

I'm motivated by uncovering challenges and solutions, building ideas, and taking action.

Inquisitive + Tweaker

Intense—Curious—Focused—Dynamic

I speak with clarifying and questioning language that includes the words *how, why, what about, what's working, evolve, edit,* and *modify.*

Leverage me when you are stuck down one path and need help seeing things differently or have a challenge where others have given up but you know there's something there worth pursuing.

I'm motivated by uncovering challenges and solutions and finding the gaps.

Instinctual + Experiential

Instinctual   Experiential

Insightful—Swift—Action Oriented—Driven

I speak with heart-based and reality-based language that includes the words *I feel, I wonder, believe, test it out, real world,* and *experiment.*

Leverage me when your thinking feels myopic and incomplete or you have a challenge or idea that has stalled and needs forward motion.

I'm motivated by feeling connected to my work and people, building ideas, and taking action.

Instinctual + Inquisitive

Instinctual   Inquisitive

Insightful—Swift—Curious

I speak with heart-based and clarifying language that includes the words *I feel, I wonder, believe, how, why, what if,* and *how about.*

Leverage me when your thinking feels myopic and incomplete or you have a challenge that needs some assumption busting and digging to find the innovation.

I'm motivated by feeling connected to my work and people and uncovering challenges and solutions.

Instinctual + Tweaker

Instinctual Tweaker

Insightful—Swift—Focused—Dynamic

I speak with heart-based and questioning language that includes the words *I feel, I wonder, believe, what's working, evolve, edit,* and *modify.*

Leverage me when your thinking feels myopic and incomplete or you have a challenge where others have given up but you know there's something there worth pursuing.

I'm motivated by feeling connected to my work and people and finding the gaps and solutions.

Risk Taker + Collaborative

Risk Taker Collaborative

Audacious—Fearless—Magnetic—Inclusive

I speak with declarative and inclusive language that includes the words *daring, impact, I know, we, together,* and *collectively.*

Leverage me when you need your thinking pushed into bolder territory or have a challenge that requires bringing together multiple perspectives.

I'm motivated by creating new opportunities and building connections between people and ideas.

Risk Taker + Imaginative

Risk Taker   Imaginative

Audacious—Fearless—Inventive—Fresh

I speak with declarative and possibility language that includes the words *daring, impact, I know, imagine, create,* and *build.*

Leverage me when you need your thinking pushed into bolder territory or have a challenge that requires the infusion of some fresh thinking.

I'm motivated by creating new opportunities and generating novel ideas.

Risk Taker + Futuristic

Risk Taker   Futuristic

Audacious—Fearless—Pioneering—Visionary

I speak with declarative and forward-motion language that includes the words *daring, impact, I know, build, next steps,* and *envision.*

Leverage me when you need your thinking pushed into bolder territory or have a challenge that requires insight around how today's work will impact tomorrow's outcomes.

I'm motivated by creating new opportunities and building new paths to the future.

Risk Taker + Fluid

Audacious—Fearless—Confident—Agile

I speak with declarative and movement-based language that includes the words *daring, impact, I know, navigate, flow,* and *try out.*

Leverage me when you need your thinking pushed into bolder territory or have a particularly messy and unclear challenge that needs clarity.

I'm motivated by creating new opportunities and creating clarity in situations and ideas.

Risk Taker + Instinctual

Audacious—Fearless—Insightful—Swift

I speak with declarative and heart-based language that includes the words *daring, impact, I know, I feel, I wonder,* and *believe.*

Leverage me when you need your thinking pushed into bolder territory or you have a challenge where current thinking feels too myopic and disconnected.

I'm motivated by creating new opportunities and feeling connected to my work and people.

Risk Taker + Inquisitive

Risk Taker   Inquisitive

Audacious—Fearless—Intense—Curious

I speak with declarative and clarifying language that includes the words *daring, impact, I know, how, why, what if,* and *how come.*

Leverage me when you need your thinking pushed into bolder territory or you have a challenge that needs some assumption busting and digging to find the innovation.

I'm motivated by creating new opportunities and uncovering challenges and solutions.

Risk Taker + Tweaker

Risk Taker   Tweaker

Audacious—Fearless—Focused—Dynamic

I speak with declarative and questioning language that includes the words *daring, impact, I know, what's working, evolve,* and *modify.*

Leverage me when you need your thinking pushed into bolder territory or you have a challenge where others have given up but you know there's something there worth pursuing.

I'm motivated by creating new opportunities and finding the gaps and solutions.

Risk Taker + Experiential

Audacious—Fearless—Action Oriented—Driven

I speak with declarative and reality-based language that includes the words *daring, impact, I know, test it out, real world,* and *experiment.*

Leverage me when you need your thinking pushed into bolder territory or you have a challenge or idea that has stalled and needs forward motion.

I'm motivated by creating new opportunities, building ideas, and taking action.

Tweaker + Experiential

Tweaker   Experiential

Focused—Driven—Action Oriented—Driven

I speak with questioning and reality-based language that includes the words *what's working, evolve, modify, test it out, real world,* and *experiment.*

Leverage me when you need someone to optimize your original ideas or have a challenge or idea that has stalled and needs forward motion.

I'm motivated by finding the gaps, solutions and building ideas and taking action.

Can you see how the magic is in the combination? The subtle nuances and uniqueness of each combination create the totality of you. How your triggers come together to impact how you add your highest value and voice to your work and life is fascinating to me. After you have read your user manual, I hope you take a moment to read the others so you can see the similarities and differences between you and the other Everyday Innovator styles.

Questions for Action

To add the details to your manual, I want you to take 30 minutes and answer the following questions about yourself. The answers will help you take what you are learning about yourself and turn it into your greatest competitive advantage. Refer to your IQE report, the content in this book, the videos in the tool kit and your user manual presented here as you answer these questions. This is the detail inside your user manual, so go deep. Don't cut yourself short by trying to answer in one sentence or with a few phrases. I also suggest word-processing the questions and your answers and keeping the summary with your icon and quick user manual.

Questions to Ask Yourself

As a _____ + _____, what unique value do I bring to my work and life?

How can I add more of my Everyday Innovator power to increase my value and voice?

How can I use my Everyday Innovator style to tackle my biggest challenges and seize opportunities?

What should I do more of to elevate my Everyday Innovator style abilities?

What should I stop doing that is sabotaging or hindering my ability to innovate?

What's one thing I want people to know about me as an _____ + _____ Everyday Innovator?

If you'd like to build the user manual for your high-performance team, I highly recommend doing #1 or #2 above (pictures or actual postcards) for everyone on your team. Then have individuals answer the questions above. Finally, bring the team together to discuss their user manuals and answers to questions above with each other.

As Jennifer Wade learned, it's powerful to have a team of Everyday Innovators with clear understandings of themselves and each other.

Chapter 8

Managing Your Dormant Trigger

Ivan with a Fluid Dormant

Up to this point, I've focused on the importance of the two main trigger points of your innovative style, playing to your strengths. However, it's important to understand your dormant trigger so you don't accidentally let it sabotage your efforts. I call it your dormant trigger because it isn't a weakness but your least powerful play. It will be more like innovating with a headwind pushing you back—you can do it, but it's tough, exhausting, and demoralizing. In that way, it's the opposite of your power triggers.

Ivan worked at a midsize IT consulting firm as director of client projects. When Ivan started, the top leadership team handed over what seemed like a daunting task, told Ivan to "let us know when you've figured it out," and took an extremely hands-off approach. Ivan remembered sitting at his desk overwhelmed by the lack of direction and the mess in front of him. He spent a few weeks spinning his wheels, not really getting anywhere. He was smart and capable and had definitely figured out sticky challenges before. Why was this so different?

When Ivan discovered that his Everyday Innovator style consisted of Inquisitive Collaborative power triggers and a Fluid dormant trigger, everything clicked. Not only was he not tapping into his power triggers, he was actively working in his dormant trigger. As a Fluid dormant, Ivan needed guardrails to innovate. He needed to better understand what was in and out of bounds so he could innovate deep in a lane. The minute Ivan figured this out, he assembled a meeting of executives and his team to create some clarity and structure around their work. When he did this, Ivan was off and running. Ivan went from feeling overwhelmed to feeling in control. He needed to adjust a few things, manage his dormant trigger, and step more into his power triggers.

My dormant trigger is Collaborative. When I first discovered this, I was angry. Anyone who knows me personally knows I love people and greatly respect and seek out the opinions of others. But what this made me realize is that, even with my love of people, I build my ideas by getting uncomfortable, leaping (Risk Taker) and testing my thinking out a bit (Experiential), and *then* sharing those ideas with others for feedback, versus someone with a Collaborative power trigger who gathers others' thinking, shares, and then formulates an idea. It's reversed. In fact, when I'm in an open brainstorming session where we start from scratch and innovate together along the way, I tend to shut down a bit. I do much better when I have a chance to generate innovative ideas, experiment with my thinking, and then attend a brainstorming meeting. Because I'm aware of this, I make sure to spend some time doing a little innovation that works for me before going to meetings like those.

I'll never forget the time someone emailed me, slightly enraged, about their dormant trigger of Risk Taker. She is an entrepreneur and felt, because she owns her own business, that she takes risks daily. That might be true, but that's not how she innovates. In fact, in her response to me she wrote, "I answered the questions on the assessment conservatively because I wasn't sure how it would turn out." Do you see it? That's someone who likes a little more certainty before taking action and tends to take small steps, one at a time. And that's okay. It doesn't make her any less innovative, just not a Risk Taker.

Ensure Your Dormant Doesn't Sabotage You

Embrace your dormant. It's not your power play and that's perfectly okay. We all have one. It doesn't mean we are any less or more, just different. My suggestion, as you read in your report, is to partner with someone that has your dormant trigger as their power trigger. That's why Laura, my right hand, is a Collaborative Tweaker. In the following chart, you'll see how each trigger manifests itself as a dormant trigger with a small piece of advice for what to do to ensure it's not holding you back.

Dormant Trigger	How It Can Hurt You	How to Overcome It
Collaborative	You prefer to have your ideas a little more thought through before sharing, sometimes keeping you in analysis paralysis or with ideas that are missing key perspectives.	Practice using language that is more inclusive and less demanding with others. Instead of "This is what I'm going to do," try "I'm considering doing this. What are your thoughts?" Practice sharing your ideas before they are fully formed.
Experiential	You may prefer to overanalyze and overthink ideas before taking action, causing innovation to stall.	Build your next idea. The first step in developing your experiential side is to build and create instead of think. Keep a drawer full of paper, pens, magazines, glue, tape, and craft materials. Every time you are in "thinking" mode, whip out your materials and build it. This action will push your mind from 2D to 3D.

Dormant Trigger	How It Can Hurt You	How to Overcome It
Fluid	You may need things more clearly defined and agreed upon, which does not always leave much room for innovative thinking because things are so set in stone.	The next time a situation arises that seems to lack the structure or defined boundaries you prefer, try shifting your perspective. Instead of thinking about the situation being out of bounds, ask yourself, *How can I expand my boundaries/ideas/ perceptions to include this undefined situation?* This will help you stretch your perceptions to embrace ambiguity and take advantage of the messiness of innovation.
Futuristic	You may look too much to the past for validation of new ideas, causing you to create solutions that aren't as relevant moving forward.	Try using future-driven language that gets your mind out of "what has been done" and into "what is possible." Try incorporating language like "what if," "could it be," and "I envision…" Starting sentences with these phrases will propel you forward.
Imaginative	You may find that you seek out too many facts and too much data before taking action, causing you to either re-create the wheel or get trapped in past thinking.	Create more moments that push your imagination. Try smashing seemingly random ideas together to get new results. Try to solve a challenge, intentionally leaving out some of the data or pieces, forcing your brain to think in a novel way to fill in the gaps.
Inquisitive	You may prefer to ask only a few questions, putting you at risk of focusing on the superficial challenge or task.	Push yourself to ask more questions every day. Every time you think you know the answer, ask three more questions. Why is that true? What is the cause of that? What else is possible?
Instinctual	You may prefer a more linear path to decision making and innovation, sometimes missing opportunities to connect the dots in different ways.	Try using language that taps into your instincts. For example, instead of saying "I know," use "I feel." Instead of "It's my understanding," say "It's my belief." This type of language will open new synapses in your mind and help you create a more instinctual way of thinking.
Risk Taker	You may not always be as comfortable with the unknown, or you may need more preparation before taking both small and big risks in work and life.	Practice small acts of risk taking daily. These successes will help you gain confidence in this area. Small risks can include speaking up in a meeting when you are nervous, picking up the phone when you are afraid of the response, or even ordering food you've never tried before.

Dormant Trigger	How It Can Hurt You	How to Overcome It
Tweaker	You may see things in a more black or white manner and want to move quickly to judgment, killing ideas too early.	Get into the mind-set of tweaking by keeping a debrief sheet at hand for everything you do. On this sheet ask yourself three simple questions: "What worked well on this effort?" "What did not work well?" "What could I change to get a better outcome?" Use your debrief sheet as your guidepost for constantly evolving your work and getting into the Tweaker mind-set.

The running joke on my team is that I don't know how to use a question mark, both in speech and in writing. As you can imagine, with Risk Taker as one of my power triggers and Collaborative as a dormant trigger, I tend to be extremely declarative in my tone. Ironically, I am totally open to others' perspectives and ideas. In fact, I welcome debate. But you wouldn't know it by my tone. I've worked hard to use more inclusive language in an effort to ensure that my dormant trigger doesn't sabotage my great work and that I include the brilliance of those around me.

Similarly, I seek people who have Collaborative as one of their power triggers. You can do the same. Find that person who has your dormant as their power trigger. You'll help each other innovate.

The impact of the dormant can show up in a lot of different ways. Is it in how you behave or in how you communicate with others? Is your job structured to set you up for success or are you constrained? Think about how you show up and where your dormant trigger may or may not be getting in the way. Then use some of the exercises mentioned in the chart above to help move further into your power triggers and away from your dormant trigger.

PART III:
SCALE INNOVATION

Chapter 9

Building High-Performance Teams

We often talk about teams as a group of people who come together for a shared purpose or in pursuit of a common goal. While that is accurate, it only scratches the surface. On a deeper level, a team is a collection of diverse individuals each seeking to both perform their task to the highest level and contribute their value to the greater good of the team.

You don't have to be a sports fanatic to see this exemplified in any team sport. In football the quarterback is looking to be the best in his role while the wide receiver is looking to be the best within his role on the team, and so on. At the same time, they are also looking to get a team win and contribute on the field whenever necessary. The punter's job is to kick the ball far down the field, putting the other team as far away from the goal line as possible, but if the opposing team catches the ball and starts gaining yards while running, he might take on some tackling responsibilities along with his teammates to prevent him from getting too far.

At the same time, the coach's job, much like a business leader's, is to make sure he helps everyone become their best, individually and as a team. High-performance teams and leaders recognize that balance and need for individual and team performance.

Alpa, the Fluid Risk Taker, and Her Team

When I was a junior consultant working at Sterling Group, a brand strategy and innovation firm based in New York City, I had this image of the business professional: how they acted, the big words they used, how they dressed. I wanted to be that buttoned-up, detail-oriented, superfirm business professional with my sharp suits and my serious demeanor. In reality, I was nothing like that person, not just because I was young, but because it wasn't me. I sort of got away with it because my matching pantsuits looked the part. But I never really settled into the profile I admired. Anyone who knows me knows I can't keep a straight face for long.

Then one day I was sitting in the office of one of my favorite project leaders, Alpa Pandya. She is brilliant and had a lot to teach me. We were discussing some options for upcoming customer research for a client.

Alpa had a way of making people feel comfortable and heard. In a moment of letting my guard and my business persona down, my real personality came out. I vividly remember having an "oh, shit" moment when I realized I wasn't keeping up appearances. But in that moment, I also realized that Alpa, instead of judging me, was actually encouraging me. She saw the value that my unique perspective brought to our work. This was in stark contrast to a few project leaders I had worked for recently who thought everything needed to be done a certain way and that was always *their* way. You have probably worked for a few people like that, too. In my opinion, that approach is a major detriment to true leadership and to teamwork.

Alpa valued uniqueness. She was brilliant and unique herself and valued it in everyone she worked with—her team, her leaders, and her clients. It's an understatement to say that, because of her brilliant mind and ability to pull the best out of everyone around her, clients wanted to work with her, and employees jumped at the chance to be on her team.

Being on her team felt like a dream come true. We were no longer a group of individual A-players, we were a high-performance, high-powered team fueled by uniqueness and diversity in thinking. We rocked!

I'm not sure Alpa realized the impact that moment in her office, or working on her team, had on me. I now know myself as an Experiential Risk Taker. I'm more of a hands-on, create-a-big-vision, leap-and-go kind of gal. From that day forward, I made sure, I, Tamara, show up every day in work and life. Everyone on Alpa's team always did.

I've since learned that Alpa is a Fluid Risk Taker. She lives it fully every day. As an individual she is a master of navigating the mess and ambiguity of a situation and turning it into innovation. Clients and teams often turn to her to help them gain clarity in the stickiest challenges. She is always willing to leap into things, learning and innovating along the way. For her, innovating and leaping are synonymous. As a leader she leverages her Fluid side to help her team find the clarity they need to move forward. The Risk Taker in her leads her team in navigating uncomfortable territory and pushes them to think bigger and bolder. And while she leverages her strengths to the max, her real brilliance is leveraging the strengths and uniqueness of everyone around her.

Being an Everyday Innovator is the foundation of great leadership and teamwork. Everyone on the team is recognized for not only their innovative contributions but also for tapping into and valuing those around them. When everyone on the team shows up as an Everyday Innovator, the team innovates, collaborates, and wins...together.

By the way, a team doesn't have to be just the people you work with directly on a specific project or in your department. Even if that's true in terms of how you work, a team is anyone you interact with in your organization or in life. Understanding how my web developer innovates helps me work with him. I have all my podcast guests take the IQE as well. If I understand how they innovate, I ensure we have a meaningful conversation that taps deep into their innovation skills and insights for my audience. I want to bring them on the podcast to showcase their brilliance, not have superficial conversations.

As I mentioned in the traps of innovation, the way to elevate your team and build a sustainable culture of innovation is through your people. Build the mind-set, create the behaviors, foster the teamwork. It's truly transformative when your team understands how they shine and contribute to the team and how each person they interact with does the same.

Here's what happens when you build and nurture a team of Everyday Innovators:

Solving Your Team's Challenges

I recently directed a simple question to my community on LinkedIn. "As a leader, what's your biggest frustration or 'wish-they'd-do-better' with your team?" The dozens of responses and direct messages I received had three common themes that are probably familiar to you.

Initiative: Stop waiting to be told what to do or for validation for what you know is the right thing to do. Be proactive, take the leap, show initiative.

Above & Beyond: Do more than complete the task at hand to a satisfactory level. Find ways to go the extra mile; elevate from standard to innovative in how you approach things.

Accountability: Don't assume that if you ignore a problem, it will go away or someone else will deal with it. Take ownership and do something about it, even if it doesn't directly impact you.

See a pattern here? As a leader, you need your teams to be stronger critical thinkers and problem solvers. You need them to be doers of innovation, to take accountability. As I mentioned previously, job descriptions are the cost of entry. To be an A-player and high-performance team, you need this next level of contribution; you need innovation and ownership. Leading a high-performance team of innovators may not completely remove your frustrations, but it will greatly improve your situation and your outcomes.

Likewise, you have to trust and believe in your teams. Groom their innovative thinking. Don't be the math teacher who instills the ideology there is only *one* way to get to the right answer.

Mortie, the Futuristic Imaginative, and His Team

Mortie and his team of 25 were together for an off-site strategy session. People flew in from across the globe, some meeting for the first time. Mortie is the team leader of the internal project group of a company in the technology reseller space. In essence, his team is responsible for operational excellence across the organization. They are a group of wickedly smart people tasked with improving the internal workings of a very large machine. Their jobs are essential to the bottom line but not as visible or glamorous as the customer-facing departments. Mortie's goal is to come away from their session as a more cohesive and collaborative team, as well as give them some tools for tackling the tough and exciting challenges they would face in the coming year.

It is clear that Mortie is an exceptional leader of a motivated team, already performing over-the-top. But this group is looking to improve. In taking the IQE, Mortie discovers he is an Imaginative Futuristic. His natural strengths lie in looking to the future for solutions and being able to create novel ideas to help get there. It's a powerful combination when leveraged. I sat next to Mortie at dinner the night before our main workshop. He said to me, "It's interesting. I've never fully understood my role as a leader in this way. When I took the IQE, it reinforced that my role is to be that visionary and push us into the future and then let my team do what they do best to help us create that future in the way that works for them."

The next day, with piles of M&Ms on the table and their Everyday Innovator styles printed on their name tags, the team sits down, eager to learn more about themselves and why I love candy-coated chocolate so much. They quickly learn that the bags of M&Ms are for an exercise they are about to experience.

Before we dive further into what happened that day, let me explain the exercise. You can gain valuable lessons from it and see the value in doing it with your team.

Step One: Break teams into "same" power triggers (one of the two power triggers overlaps). For example, in one group, everyone in the group has an Inquisitive power trigger. In another group, everyone has an Imaginative power trigger. A third group has Collaborative power triggers. Usually, the group consists of 5 to 6 participants.

Step Two: Using the bags of M&Ms (I suggest a large bag of M&Ms per table), the group has 10 minutes to build a house.

Step Three: Share and debrief each group's creations and experience. This is where it gets interesting. There are clear differences in how each group behaves—some strengths and some weaknesses—and the houses they create.

Step Four: Reassemble groups into "diverse" teams. The Everyday Innovator styles in a group should be as different as possible. You may have one Fluid Tweaker, an Inquisitive Collaborative, a Risk Taker Experiential, a Futurisitic Imaginative, and so on. There may be some overlap, but the goal is to make them as diverse as possible.

Step Five: New teams must pick a built house and transform it into a rocket ship. They are not allowed to start from scratch or wipe the slate clean. As in real life, they must use what they have and transform it into something new within 10 minutes.

Note: I tend to be flexible on the time. If the teams are done early, I'm comfortable calling time. If the energy is high, I'm also comfortable extending it by a few minutes. It shouldn't go on too long because, as in life, we have limited resources and time.

Step Six: Share and debrief. This is where the real insights happen. Individuals discover how they shine and add value, and teams recognize the power of diversity in thinking.

Note of caution: Sometimes moving into the diverse teams is an uncomfortable and challenging experience for your team. That's okay; a little discomfort and awkward silence is a part of the process. As Linda from a global hotel chain told me after doing this exercise with her team, "When we were in similar groups, it was fun and the energy was high, but the solutions were average at best. When we were in diverse groups, at first, it was difficult. We had to better understand how to collaborate and communicate, to respect the others' thinking. But when we got over that hurdle, the ideas were 10 times more powerful."

Step Seven: Have each participant take a moment to write down:
- what they learned about themselves
- what they learned about their teammates
- how they can better utilize their innovation superpowers in the work they do
- how they can better leverage their team, given their various Everyday Innovator styles

Use their answers to foster a group conversation.

As you can imagine, this is a very powerful exercise. People learn a lot about themselves and others in a 60-minute period. The team begins to recognize how each member adds value. They discover how they can use their various styles of innovation to solve their biggest challenges and create new opportunities.

During step seven, our final debrief, Mortie puts his Imaginative Futuristic to work. He turns to the group and says, "Hey, what's our biggest day-to-day challenge?"

From the back of the room, someone shouts, "Getting what we need, the documents, the data. It's a constant struggle to get everything we need to do our jobs."

Everyone in the group nods in sync. Clearly, this is not the first time they've discussed this issue.

I smile because these are the types of nagging challenges that seem insurmountable in their continuous nature until you unleash your innovation superpowers.

Then something fascinating happens. First, Mortie, with his ability to turn today's challenges into tomorrow's solutions, says, "What if we are solving the wrong challenge? If we started differently, would we end differently?" That is the Imaginative side crafting a novel approach to their challenge.

Next, Isaak, a Collaborative Tweaker, taps the power of his Everyday Innovator style and takes what Mortie started and runs with it, bringing the group along for the ride.

Isaak says, "To add to what you are saying, what if we stop solving that one and, instead, solve how we start every project with everything we need up-front? Where do you guys think that could take us?" In true Tweaker form, he finds the innovation by slightly adjusting what Mortie said. And in his Collaborative powers, he then pushes the question back to the team to gather their perspectives.

Before I know it, there is a slight murmur in the room as the team begins to tackle their biggest challenge with a new innovative lens.

Cool, right?! The truth is I didn't really do much. All I did was bring them a framework that helped them unlock what was already inside and give them a platform to unleash it. With the right knowledge and environment, amazing things are possible.

Here's what can happen when everyone on the team unlocks their Everyday Innovator:

#1: Tap the Power of Diversity in Thinking

"Diversity of thought is the very bedrock of innovation. When you get a group of people with different cognitive styles, perspectives, and experiences together, you create an environment where innovation naturally thrives. You strengthen ideas and create innovation that is thoughtful, relevant, and meaningful. Innovation is also more likely to be *implemented* when created by a group with diverse mind-sets. Everyone becomes a stakeholder and the innovation reflects the views of different constituencies. It's more wholistic—that's why it works."—Kelly McDonald, Collaborative Instinctual and author of the book *How to Work With and Lead People Not Like You*

Several recent studies show that teams that have and leverage diverse thinking are smarter. Diversity in thinking leads to more inquiry, challenging of one another, and different perspectives. This leads to more wholly thought out work output.[1] Basically, interacting with people unlike you forces you out of your bubble, challenges your biases, and helps you fill the holes in your thinking. All you have to do is be open to it. This is why ideas that come from birds of a feather tend to die, but those that come from diverse thinking thrive. Diversity in thinking can come from a partnership of two, a team, or across your organization.

And it goes even deeper. Alison Reynolds from the UK's

Ashridge Business School and David Lewis, director of London Business School's Senior Executive Program, ran a series of studies to better understand how diversity impacted a team's performance, in particular their ability to be innovative and productive. Their findings were fascinating. It turns out, while race, gender, and age are important in creating diversity in a company, they did not impact the team's ability to be innovative and productive. In discovering this, it begged the question of what did. Teams with cognitive diversity performed smarter and stronger. Cognitive diversity is defined as "differences in perspective or information processing styles. It is not predicted by factors such as gender, ethnicity, or age," [2] although one could argue that those factors lead to different thinking styles purely because those individuals come from different vantage points and experience. The point is to dig deeper, look beyond the surface, and tap into the cognitive differences that bring powerful diversity. This is exactly what we are talking about with the unique Everyday Innovator styles on your team.

Power of Two: Joel, Cameron, and the Red Wagon

Joel's mom was a visionary. When he was little, she made the most amazing whole-grain pancakes from scratch. His mom thought the world needed more healthy options, so when Joel was eight, she set him up with a little red wagon and a bunch of pancake mixes measured out in brown paper bags that he could take door-to-door to sell his mom's amazing recipe.

Fast-forward to Joel's adulthood, and Mom's recipe is now Kodiak Cakes, sold on the shelves of Costco, Target, and other stores. You may recognize them for their protein pancake mix or delicious muffin mix. But Kodiak's route to success wasn't linear.

It involved many twists and turns. In fact, originally Joel's brother, John, was running the company. It was small and sold mostly in gift shops. In 1987, John wanted to go back to school and asked Joel if he would take over the business. Here is Joel, an Inquisitive Tweaker, taking over a mediocre business with one product on the shelf in a seriously declining category that hasn't seen any real innovation or excitement in decades. Think about the breakfast section of the grocery store for a minute. Anything new and exciting happening? Nope, same old cereal, oatmeal, and pancake mixes...that is, until Kodiak came along.

When I interviewed Joel Clark, CEO of Kodiak, and Cameron Smith, cofounder and president, for my podcast, I asked them about why they would bother to waste their energy on a declining category totally lacking in innovation. Their answer says it all and speaks to their teamwork and commitment to being Everyday Innovators.

> "Even buyers would tell us back then, 'You know, not that many people are making pancakes anymore.' Kind of crazy, looking back. The launch of a whole entire business in a category that's not growing, that's not exciting to buyers and consumers, and isn't very big. But we've found that it's a sweet spot for us, [a] category's [that] kind of declining. In our minds, it's an opportunity because it means that the category hasn't seen any real innovation. It's why we went into frozen waffles. We see how we can bring people back to the category instead of stealing dollars from someone else."

You can read their Everyday Innovator styles in their answers.

Together, Joel and Cameron have changed the whole-grain game. Joel, as an Inquisitive Tweaker, challenges assumptions and figures out how to elevate what exists, and Cameron, as a

Collaborative Risk Taker, connects all the various pieces to find innovation and thinks big in how to approach the category. That's the power of strong and diverse collaboration. Yes, they are individually intelligent and innovative. Their real power comes from respecting and leveraging their diverse thinking styles. If you listen to episode 1789 of *Inside LaunchStreet,* you'll hear how diverse and complementary they are. It's in their diversity that they found a magical combination for tremendous success and growth.

Power of Team: Sean, Energy, and Engineers

Sean Richard, an innovation leader at Schneider Electric, a leading company in the public energy sector, recognizes the importance of diversity across teams. After having the initial team of roughly 150 leaders take the IQE, one of the first things we did together was create a heat map to understand how the team innovates together. The first thing Sean pointed out as we looked at the heat map is the diversity of innovative thinking on his teams. The heat map showed myriad Everyday Innovator styles. In fact, they had at least 21 of the 36 style combinations just in the teams we surveyed.

Sean wasn't just looking for hot spots of innovation, he was seeking to understand how to leverage and build high-performing teams by tapping everyone's diverse Everyday Innovator styles. He knows everyone has the innovation magic, even in the places you least expect it. Which is why he implemented the IQE assessment and tool kit with the Energy Engineering Group. As you can imagine, this is a group of high-level smart people, but they aren't typically seen as the innovators. He knows they bring a set of diverse thinking and wants them to dig deeper than their day-to-day work. Sometimes tapping the diversity in your teams is all about helping them realize their value beyond the obvious. Armed with their Everyday Innovator styles, the Energy Engineering Group and multiple other teams at Schneider are leveraging diversity to build a stronger company and more meaningful solutions for their clients. This is part of the reason why they are leading the industry in times of massive change and uncertainty.

#2: Create Space for Vulnerability and Trust

When David Marquet was given command of the USS *Santa Fe*, a nuclear submarine, he realized he had one massive challenge. Although he was an incredibly intelligent and experienced leader, he had no experience with this type of submarine. In an environment where "you are supposed to know the answers and give commands," he didn't. So he went on board expecting to have to rely on his crew to know their jobs and the ship. David, wanting to get up to speed, went around asking the crew about the equipment. As he told me in an Inside *LaunchStreet* podcast (episode 1840) interview:

"Nine times out of 10, they'd know, but the tenth one wouldn't. They'd say, 'Oh, I forgot.' And then everyone would look at me because I was supposed to know the answer. But, of course, I didn't know. And I had this moment where I wanted to pretend, but I didn't. Maybe something weird was going on in my head that day, so I said, 'I don't know either.' They are looking at me; I'm looking at them. 'Let's go find out together.'"

This was a turning point in David's leadership of the USS *Santa Fe*. As an Inquisitive Risk Taker, David was open to digging into what he didn't understand and was willing to get uncomfortable and attempt a more daring approach to leadership. In that moment, he recognized the team he was leading brought more than just their skills or textbook knowledge. If given the room, they brought critical thinking and teamwork. David goes on to share many stories of "experimentations" his crew did to better understand the capabilities and power of the submarine for which they were responsible. But none of that could have happened if David hadn't given his crew the space to be vulnerable. Vulnerability takes trust: trust that we value and respect each other; trust that you will be heard; trust that if you don't know or have a wild idea, you won't be penalized for it.

Google spent two years studying teams. One of the top five traits they found was teams that thrive have psychological safety.[3] That means the individuals on the team felt safe enough to be vulnerable and take risks. They also found that teams with psychological safety were more likely to tap diverse thinking.

How do you get to psychological safety and what does it have to do with being innovative? In deploying the IQE to hundreds of teams across the world, we discovered that the underpinning of psychological safety is respect and value. As David discovered, when you value your team, you create room to be wrong, to experiment, and to take risks. It's that simple: recognize and value the innovative mind each person on the team brings and you'll create the important foundation of vulnerability and trust. With those two characteristics, anything is possible.

When you have your team take the IQE and use that knowledge to help them shine individually, and then foster team performance, you are making a financial and time investment in them. Plus, you are telling them you value and respect what they bring to the table. That feeling goes a long way toward keeping your team engaged and invested.

After your team has taken the IQE assessment and read the book, there's one conversation that helps them shed the layers of needing to look right and perfect and get to this deep layer of respect. It's in discussing how each individual shines and causes friction. Discuss the amazing and the frustrating side. If you talk only about the good things, the frustrations will fester. And if you focus on the frustrations, it becomes a bitch session. But in discussing both, you get real and raw, and that's where you find vulnerability and trust. It's not about making anyone right or wrong but about bringing to light the differences and the uniqueness in the room. From that point, everything is possible.

The following chart shows how each power trigger adds value and causes friction. I suggest leading this discussion with "why" the group is having this convesation. I've heard leaders make statements such as:

- "We have some big challenges up ahead and it's important that we set ourselves up for success by discovering how to work as the highest performing team possible."
- "We have an incredible group of people in the room, but an underlying friction has kept us from working well as a team. Today is about removing that friction and recognizing how each of us plays a key role on the team."
- "We have achieved some incredible goals this past year. Now I want to look into the future and that means upping our game even more. To do that we need to take a deep breath and focus on how to become the strongest team possible."
- "Each person in this room brings incredible value to the team. But there is some distrust and miscommunication that has gotten in the way of being the team we need to be to tackle what's ahead for us. Today is about removing those layers, building trust, and figuring out how to collaborate and win."

When your "why" is established, a few key conversation starters will ignite a robust dialogue that pulls back the invisible layers that hinder trust, respect, and vulnerability. Whatever your "why" is, state it upfront to help your team understand this exercise is meant to support and strengthen their efforts, not penalize them. They can't read your mind, so delineate your intentions to help get everyone on the same page and have the conversation through the right lens.

Conversation starters:

How They Shine:

Their answers need to be specific about individual people. If they start with generalities, keep asking them questions until they become more specific. It may take a few rounds for them to truly understand how to have this conversation.

- Give me some specific examples of how your teammates have brought their Everyday Innovator styles to add value to you and the work you all do.
- Tell me how someone on your team has shined in the last few weeks.
- Give me an example how someone on this team has added value or made your work better in the past few weeks.

How They Cause Friction:

- How do you think, given how you innovate, you might cause friction with others on your team?
- Now that you recognize some of that friction you feel is because your teammates are coming from different perspectives, how can you turn that friction into an advantage?
- What will you do differently the next time you feel that friction with your teammate?

When you've set your "why" and engage in a few key conversation starters, you are on your way to creating space for vulnerability. When there is space for vulnerability, you create space for tapping diversity in thinking as well.

As I mentioned previously, it's important that everyone on your team knows their IQE so they can study and understand the following chart (and all the others in this book). The more your team understands why their ability to innovate matters and how to view those around them for what each team member brings to the table, the more productive and powerful the results.

	Add Value	Cause Friction
Collaborative	Brings in lots of viewpoints; easily gets buy-in from others; builds teams	Sometimes talks to too many people; can be viewed as slowing down the process because they need so much input
Experiential	Makes it real so people can see it, experience it; brings ideas to life	Seen as moving too fast or too impulsive; people can feel left behind
Fluid	Stays nimble during change; has a figure-it-out mind-set; able to find clarity in sticky and messy situations	Can create too many options; looks distracted and disorganized to others; hard to follow
Futuristic	Sees possibilities; can see how one change impacts the future; solves problems for the future	Trouble communicating long-term visions; ideas can be seen as not grounded in today's realities
Imaginative	Imaginative ideas; fills in the blank spaces for people; adds fresh perspective to stale thinking	Can be "dreamers"; others lack the proof in their ideas; can be viewed as unrealistic
Inquisitive	Challenges assumptions holding people back; digs deep to find root of issues	Viewed as annoying or not on board; stays in inquiry and can't move forward

	Add Value	Cause Friction
Instinctual	Connects dots and finds meaningful patterns; finds new meaning in old things	Viewed as disengaged or unable to explain thinking; viewed as too haphazard
Risk Taker	Challenges small ideas; bold, early adopter, willing to get uncomfortable; people will follow them	Makes others uncomfortable; seen as pushing too hard, too soon; can be viewed as reckless
Tweaker	Modifies; makes better; adds improvements	Won't stop modifying; difficulty finalizing and completing tasks

#3: Elevate Investment & Engagement

I've had the pleasure of speaking with Alex Goryachev, an Imaginative Inquisitive Everyday Innovator and the managing director of the Cisco Innovation Centers, several times. He's full of incredible insights on building cultures of innovation. However, the last time we spoke, he told me a story that, while surprising, also highlights the importance of the innovation right in front of you.

In his role as managing director of Cisco Innovation Centers, he oversees multiple processes that help discover and fund innovation throughout the world. Originally, the system was set up to find outside entrepreneurs with innovative ideas and fund and support them. This was a way of infusing new thinking into the very large system that is a company of Cisco's size. They did this by creating submission contests. One day, a daring Cisco employee (guessing she was a Risk Taker Inquisitive) contacted Alex and bluntly asked him, "So, in order for you to pay attention to my idea, should I quit Cisco?" The lightbulb went off for Alex. He realized that while they were going far and wide in search of innovation lands, they were ignoring the innovation in their backyard. The Imaginative Inquisitive in him sat back, began to question the entire program, and then went to HR with a novel approach that would seek to tap the power of the tens of thousands of employees already in the Cisco family.

Kudos to Alex for recognizing the importance of this person's comment and to Cisco for acting on it. To say that this shift has been a success is an understatement. As you can imagine, treating your own team like innovators ups engagement, performance, innovation, and your bottom line.

Great outcomes begin with people who are invested and engaged with their work. The stats about employee engagement are abysmal. Something to the effect of 75 percent of people are disengaged. That's most of your team. In our work with teams, one of the most dramatic transformations we've seen in executing the IQE system is the transformation from "this is just a job" to "I'm fully invested." When everyone is fully engaged and invested, the team transforms from a group of underleveraged A-players doing their own thing to a high-performing team that is proactive and innovative. They become "team-motivated," invested in the outcomes above and beyond their personal gain. It's about what the team is trying to accomplish and the outcomes that serve the project. When people feel valued and heard, they don't play territorial games and feel the need to outshine their teammates. Instead, their eye is on the greater team prize.

#4: Build Real Collaboration That Wins

Sheila and her team work at one of the largest fast food companies in the world. As the industry title states, things move quickly. But Sheila had an elephant in the room she needed to address. She had three teams—marketing, innovation, and research and development—that needed to work together if she wanted to deliver results that didn't just keep up with but beat the competition.

However, they weren't working as well together as they should. The "We do all the work, what do they do?" or "We know better" mind-set had taken hold and created silos, and those silos hindered their performance. This is common and, I have no doubt, you've experienced this with your teams as well. Sheila knew she couldn't let this fester, so she took action. Using our Facilitator's Guide and Toolkit, she facilitated a training session with all the teams. Each person took the IQE and discovered how they innovate, and as a team they came together to debrief their results with exercises Sheila and I crafted specifically given her challenge.

When I touched base with Sheila later, she told me something I'll never forget. She said,

What's important to recognize here is that my team came in skeptical. They love learning about themselves, but they knew this was going to be about us as a team, so there were several arms crossed when we started. But by the end, everyone was leaning in to each other. Two important things came out of this meeting. First, we all now understand how to bring our best selves to work, and, personally, that's really powerful. More important for us, in discussing how each style can support their teammates, we got to a place where real collaboration is possible. We even created new ways to support and leverage the innovation on the team. And in our world, that collaboration means actions—creating new products, testing them out, moving them forward in the system.

Sheila, a Collaborative Imaginative, and her team of diverse Everyday Innovators discovered how to tap the power of the IQE to respect, communicate, collaborate, and win—together.

#5: Create the Ultimate Team-mance

Footers Catering is a vibrant, bright office space. The moment you walk through the doors, you can feel the buzz of happiness around you. The energy in this place is infectious, and soon you find yourself smiling along with everyone in the company. You know it when you see it—a team that loves what they do and doing it together. This is the company Anthony Lambatos has created. I call it a "team-mance." It's kind of like that pop culture portmanteau *bro-mance* or *girl-mance*, when two people absolutely adore each other in a platonic way. Take that to the team level and you have team-mance, a team that absolutely loves working together. It doesn't mean they are all the same; quite the opposite. It means they respect, appreciate, and work together like a winning football team. They recognize and value that each person in the company brings a diverse set of skills, a unique way of innovating, and a strong voice.

As the president and a Collaborative Tweaker, Anthony works hard to ensure the culture of innovation Footers Catering is felt and acted on daily. One of the first things I noticed, aside from the bright teal walls, is that each person has their Everyday Innovator styles front and center, taped to their office door. And on the wall of the main hallway, where everyone walks multiple times a day, is a heat map of the entire organization. "Every time I walk down the hall I'm reminded of the innovation power on this team. Kara is an Inquisitive Collaborative, so I'll go to her when I'm stuck and can't seem to figure out how to get to the heart of a problem I'm facing. When I can't seem to get beyond incremental, I see Stephanie for her Futuristic Collaborative approach that brings more forward-thinking ideas to the table."

"When creating a committee, I'll be sure to get a mix of Everyday Innovators so we can have robust discussions and generate innovation that sticks."

Anthony and his team have created a culture so strong and successful the company continues to grow in revenue and in recognition. Other hospitality and event companies pay to tour Footers and learn how to improve the culture in their companies. In fact, learning the lessons of how they built their culture is so sought after, Anthony had to start an entire consulting arm just to meet that demand.

He understands that to avoid launch-and-abandon techniques he has to ignite innovation and keep the momentum going. In putting the heat map on the wall, Everyday Innovator styles on every door, and continually discussing their innovation superpowers, the innovation at Footers is flowing daily.

Chapter 10

The Wheel of Innovation

Somehow, I got talked into doing a 150-mile bike ride for charity with a friend. At the time I didn't own a bike, let alone ride on a regular basis. But I'm always up for a challenge, so I borrowed my neighbor's road bike, purchased a few energy chews, and went for it. With 75 miles to go on day one and a 90-degree temperature hitting my back, I wasn't sure if I'd made the right decision. About 35 miles in, I was definitely questioning my life choices. Each turn of the wheel felt like its own struggle. I knew I was out of practice, but this felt clunkier and harder than I expected it would. Eventually, I made my way to a resting stop that included a bike repair station. After falling over in front of a crowd of a few hundred expert bikers because I couldn't unclip my feet from the pedals before the bike stopped, I walked my weary body and bike over to the repair station. I told them how hard and clunky every turn felt. They took one look at the front wheel and said, "Oh, your wheel is out of balance and has pebbles in it, making it an awkward shape." I swear, the minute they fixed my front wheel, it was as if my bike was transformed into a speed racer machine. Don't get me wrong, the remaining miles were tough; but with a well-balanced wheel, I moved forward with speed and efficiency (and lots of sore muscles) I didn't know I had.

As you know from driving or riding your own bike, a balanced wheel will take you far, and you are able to move forward easily. However, an imbalanced wheel can stop you in your tracks.

The wheel of innovation is no different. A well-balanced wheel full of diverse Everyday Innovators will go farther, faster, and leave others in the dust. An innovation wheel totally out of balance will go forward slowly, with lots of jarring stops and starts, or may suffer a blowout.

Balanced Wheels:

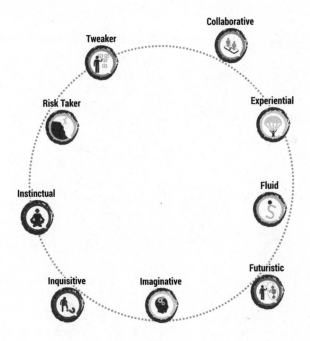

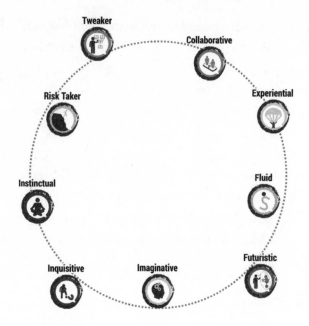

Imbalanced Wheels:

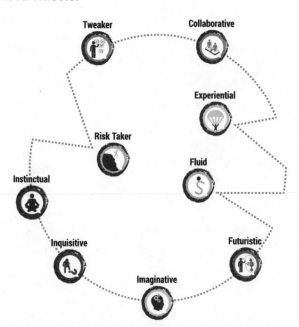

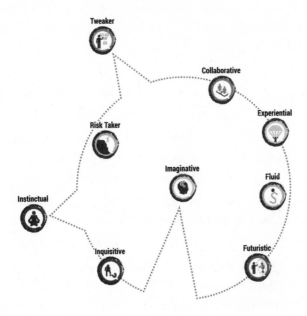

The difference is in the visual. Your wheel, or team, doesn't need to be exactly even across all triggers, but you do want it to have relative balance. When you have a balanced wheel, with each spoke on the wheel bringing their best selves and those spokes connected through respect and collaboration, the momentum is inevitable. Your wheel is your competitive advantage. It's your access to all types, styles, and approaches to solve your challenges and unearth opportunities.

Interestingly, what I've also identified in having teams across industries, ranging from healthcare to IT to consumer products to banking, take the IQE is that each industry or job sector has its own unique pattern. That pattern tells me a lot about a team— the type of people attracted to that work, the type of people a company hires, their strengths as a team, their weaknesses as a team. Inevitably, their greatest strengths as a team correlate directly to their predominant innovation triggers. The same is true on the flip side. A predominance of one particular dormant trigger or a power trigger that is missing completely can be seen in their weaknesses.

If you are the adventurous one taking the IQE before your team, I have a quick and fun observational exercise for you. Through the week, pay attention to how your group operates as a team. Take note of how you behave together. Are you really solid, inclusive of each other? Does your team have a tough time when a last-minute curveball hits them? No judgment, just observation. After the rest of your team takes the IQE and you learn their Everyday Innovator styles, check how closely your observations match your team's wheel. What Everyday Innovator styles do you have on your team? Use the next chart to understand how the styles correlate. In understanding the behaviors of your team, you can better understand how to leverage your innovation strengths and how to overcome your weaknesses.

Trigger	If Dominant Power	If Missing Trigger
Collaborative	Builds strong relationships across the team, works well with cross-functional teams to get things done, tends to take all perspectives into account	Lots of lone wolves working in silos, struggle to work with and connect with others, tendency to push their thinking on others before listening
Experiential	Move to action immediately; things get done, fast; prefer fewer meetings and more doing	Gets stuck in analysis paralysis; lots of conversations, not a lot of action
Fluid	Conversations and work lack direction	Rebel when structure is imposed on them
Futuristic	Lots of energy for brainstorming, not for implementation	Need lots of data before making a decision
Imaginative	Always chasing the next best thing	Constantly repeats past ideas; gets trapped in regurgitating information without new insights

Trigger	If Dominant Power	If Missing Trigger
Inquisitive	Rarely ready to move forward because there are more questions to ask	Conversations are superficial, people do as told
Instinctual	Lots of cool insights and patterns, not a lot of applicable ideas	Everything is done in a linear process, following the project management chart to a T
Risk Taker	A lot of initiation, not a lot of follow-through because no one thought that far ahead	Plays it safe; likes to talk themselves out of bolder actions
Tweaker	Things are never final, always in an evolutionary state	Team gives up after the first try

The Impact of Balance & Imbalance

I've worked with a lot of teams, with both balanced and imbalanced wheels of innovation. Now I recognize that teams come in all shapes and sizes. You may have a team of 50, where all Everyday Innovator styles are represented, or you may not. This isn't to say you have to have a team that includes all nine triggers. Your size simply may not make that feasible. However, in learning how to balance your wheel, here are three stories that are compilations of real-world teams, with both balance and imbalance and of various sizes. I think regardless of your situation, you'll find some valuable lessons in all of them.

Paulina's team is the hub of the organization. As the project managers of a thriving logistics software company, her 12-person team is spread across the company, interacting with all levels of the organization to ensure projects meet their deadlines. To leverage the fact that they have a relatively balanced wheel of Everyday Innovators, the team meets weekly to discuss their projects and gather advice from one another. This works brilliantly because when Vincent, a Risk Taker Imaginative, struggles with some of the minute details of his projects, Quinn, a Tweaker Experiential, can coach him in some of those small steps that might make a huge impact. When Ivanna, an Instinctual Fluid, listens to everyone talk, she then adds tremendous value to the conversation by sharing with the team how she sees the patterns and insights that connect all the projects they are working on. And Jessica, a Collaborative Futuristic, leans on Yen, an Inquisitive Tweaker, when she can't seem to figure out the right questions to ask her team to get better results.

Paulina discovered that using their team meetings as a way to tap the diverse Everyday Innovator styles helps each of them perform better in their work when they aren't together. She also noticed how she finds her team randomly connecting in the hallways to "bounce stuff off each other" more often. And when they start discussing their own internal processes and solutions, the entire team comes together, tackling their challenges from all innovation angles, making the solutions they create robust and thoughtful.

When it comes to being a high-performing team of innovators, Paulina and her team are focused on continually bringing out the best in themselves and leveraging those around them. Every day, they make use of LaunchStreet's online tools to keep the innovation momentum going.

Below is the innovation wheel I presented in the beginning of the book that showed the different styles of innovation in summary. Imagine for a moment when a solution is created with this type of balanced wheel. What it would be like if your team, like Paulina's, could tackle and create solutions from all angles?

For an example of how missing parts of the wheel can lead to holes in thinking and solutions and what you can do about it, let's look at a team that needed some work. Terry Lee found that, individually, her team was very skilled; however, as a team, they seemed to have some gaps that were keeping them from delivering

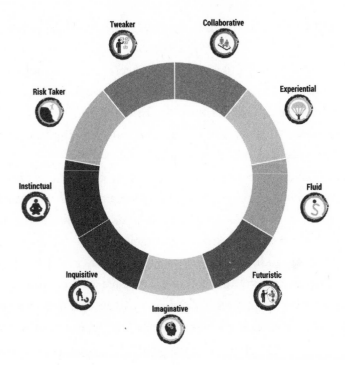

outstanding work to their clients. Her clients were counting on her team of business consultants to help them identify and move past the hurdles that were keeping them from growing revenues. What drew Terry Lee and her team to their work was digging into the complexities of their clients' challenges. But lately it felt as if her team's solutions were missing the mark.

When Terry Lee examined their wheel of Everyday Innovator styles, it became apparent why. They were heavy on the Inquisitive, which is great for digging deep and challenging assumptions, and on Risk Taker, which meant bold thinking and willingness to chart new territory, but they were completely missing Experiential and Fluid. This meant a lack of real-world innovation, a drive to test and experiment with their thinking and not always being able to find the clarity in the mess and uncertainty their clients were often facing. Terry Lee quickly went to work to fix this and hired specifically for those missing power triggers. She hired four new consultants who matched those profiles and integrated them into the larger team as soon as possible. In doing this, she created a well-balanced wheel of innovation. The team had always debated ideas, and now those debates were more robust.

The challenge, recognized by Terry Lee, disappeared because the gaps they had in their thinking no longer existed. She fought the desire to hire birds of a feather and, in doing so, found that her balanced wheel translated into measurable results.

Taking an additional step forward, Terry Lee and her team have their Everyday Innovator styles printed and on display in the main hallway, in their offices, and in their email signatures, so they keep innovation front and center. Furthermore, when they gather, either virtually or live, they start with an IQE exercise so the power of the team is tapped on a regular basis. Tipping the scale in another direction, how can you create balance when your staff is limited in numbers?

Sanjay and his team of five are small but mighty. As the regional marketing team for a hotel chain, they are responsible for all the local marketing efforts from online advertising to live promotions. Often their work involves 48-hour deadlines as they work to take advantage of local events and news in their marketing campaigns. Sanjay does not have the resources for a higher head count, so everyone on the team needs to be high-performing. For the most part, the team works as a well-oiled machine, with each team member performing their job to the best of their ability and jumping in to help their colleagues on urgent projects.

However, the team recently realized they have a few gaps in

their approach to their campaigns. No one on the team has a Futuristic or an Instinctual power trigger in their Everyday Innovator styles. In fact, four of the five have a Tweaker power trigger, making them overly strong in this area. Because of this, the team and their work sometimes miss taking into consideration the long-term implications as they work to turn things around quickly. It also means they don't always see how the various projects connect to each other.

In an ideal world, Sanjay would get approval to hire more people so he could create a more balanced wheel and be able to spread out the workload. But that's not his reality, and Sanjay had to figure out how to fill the gaps.

After working with a LaunchStreet expert, Sanjay created a plan that would allow him to tap the innovation strengths of his team as well as ensure that imbalances don't hinder their work efforts. Sanjay and his team now have a copy of the Everyday Innovator styles exercises one-pager (page 101) pinned to each of their cubes. At the top is the sentence "Seek the power of the team" to remind everyone to pop their heads up and ask their diverse teammates for help, to brainstorm, or simply to talk out something they are working on. The Futuristic and Instinctual power trigger rows are highlighted. The team knows that after they've tapped the power of their teammates, the final step is to ensure there are no holes. To achieve this, they are encouraged to do some of the exercises on the sheet that aren't represented on their team, specifically Futuristic and Instinctual. In doing this, they were able to ensure the gaps didn't sabotage their work; in fact, it strengthened it. Doing so gave them a chance to think as a different Everyday Innovator for a moment and ensure all their hard work wasn't being sabotaged simply because they missed one perspective.

An imbalanced wheel of innovation may have you and/or your team stuck in a rut and moving forward sluggishly, while a balanced, complete wheel will supercharge your momentum and results. Rest assured, there are ways to work around and with your circumstances to create a wheel as close to balanced as possible.

Chapter 11

Be a Leader of Innovation

Overcoming "They Syndrome"

Now that you've released your ability to innovate into the world, you may be wondering, *How do I communicate in a way that makes others stand up and pay attention?* It's painful to feel as if your innovative contributions are always shut down. It's even worse to have them heard and avoided. However, before you read on, take into consideration that while someone else is squelching your innovative ideas, it's not their responsibility to do something about it; it's yours. I call it the "they syndrome." It shows up as "They don't get it," "They don't see it," or "They are the reason I am stuck." If the word *they* is thrown around a lot, I know instantly that the individual or team I'm dealing with lacks accountability. Don't feel bad about it and no one is judging you. Be aware it happens; we've all been there. "They syndrome" sneaks up on you.

Ultimately, you are the innovator. It's your job to get others along the innovation journey with you. This became incredibly apparent to me several years ago when I suffered from a bad case of "they syndrome."

A large baby care brand hired me to help them reinvent baby care. Baby wipes, shampoo, baby powder—this category hadn't seen any real innovation in years.

I assembled my A-team of consultants. We kicked off the project with a bang, and for six months we were out there shopping at baby stores, testing bath products, and playing with toys. For the first time in the company's history, we talked to dads about their needs. After six months of hard work, my team created a range of new product ideas we thought would transform the baby care category. We had close-in ideas they could implement immediately and further-out ideas that would take them into new territories. For our final presentation, my team and I flew to the client's headquarters for the big meeting. We shuffled into the CEO's conference room. I'll never forget—it had a big wood table that took up most of the room and those pink pastel chairs that had been there since the '70s. The walls were lined with oil paintings of CEOs past, none of them smiling. I'm standing at the podium with my team looking out at the room. To my right is my client and then his boss. After that the table is filled with all the bigwigs.

I'm beaming with pride as my team starts to go through their ideas. But as they are talking, I can hear this whispering over to my right. It's my client's boss. I don't remember his name, but I can tell you he had a mustache so large it moved when he spoke. With every idea, he would lean in to my client and whisper comments like "Didn't Joan in R&D try that in 1998 and we shelved it?" "Didn't a competitor launch that and it failed?" "Didn't another consultant give us a similar idea we didn't like?" He squashed the life out of every idea.

That was the longest, angriest plane ride home. I went through the 12 steps of rage of the "they syndrome."

At first, I was generally incredulous. I thought, *Why did they hire us if they weren't going to listen to our ideas?*

Then I went on to Mustache Man. *How dare he. He's been doing his job too long and shouldn't have anything to do with innovation. When I get off this plane I'm going to call my client and tell him someone should fire Mustache Man.*

Next, I moved on to my client. I raged: *If he can't get buy-in from the people we need to implement these ideas, he shouldn't be running innovation projects. When I get off this plane, I'm going to call him and tell him he should be fired.*

Finally, I moved on to my poor team: *They are not the team I thought they were. They totally snowed me. Their ideas sucked, and I should never have let them be presented. I'm going to fire all of them before we hit baggage claim.*

Fortunately for everyone, by the time we landed, I realized who was really at fault. It wasn't the clients or my team; it was me. We had spent six months pushing the limits of possibilities and stretching our thinking, and then we shuffled into this room with key decisions makers and expected them to get it.

Let me be very clear here. Your clients aren't you. Whoever is sitting across the table from you doesn't have your experiences or passion. They haven't been thinking about your new idea or solution the way you have. Furthermore, my expectation that the ideas and a beautiful presentation would do the talking for me was false. There I was pushing my brilliance onto the people in the room. Do you like it when someone else pushes their ideas onto you? No, of course not, and neither did the people in that room. It didn't matter how brilliant or transformative my team's ideas were, they were met with a big, thick, invisible brick wall.

Mustache Man taught me a very valuable lessons that day; it transformed how I communicate and teach others to communicate. He taught me that innovation has its own language, and in that language you can either shut down or speed up the momentum of innovation.

He helped me to create the Language of Innovation method. The elements of this are the most utilized lessons in our tool kit. They include: Open Questions, Pain and Possibilities, and What's in It for Them. I share them here with you because, as I discovered, if you change your language, you change your outcomes.

Open Questions

Let me use an everyday object like a water bottle to share this lesson with you. Let's say I have an idea for a revolutionary water bottle. In the next all-team meeting, I excitedly share this idea by putting up a slide and telling you and the team:

I've got this new water bottle idea totally unlike the one we sell now. This one has a built-in thumb sensor so it knows what vitamins you need and adds them to the water. It also has a temperature setting so it cools down when it's too hot and vice versa. And because it knows your thumbprint, it doesn't let anyone else open up the cap but you. *What do you think?*

When I share this story with groups, the response is always the same. Maybe three or four people in the room smile and say "Let's do it" while the remaining dozens, or even thousands, stare blankly at me. This is what happens to you when you don't use the language of innovation to communicate.

Let's break down what's happening here and then give you the shift in language that is going to drastically change your outcomes for the better.

First, did you feel like I was trying to convince you? The answer should be yes. How did it feel? Probably not great. I'm like an idea pusher and all the energy between us is me exerting it heavily toward you. When you present your thinking in this way, you shut down the other person's engagement. There's no room for their opinions or perspectives. You probably don't intend to do this. I know I didn't, but it's how it comes across.

Second, and this is the most important part, when you end your statement or presentation with statements such as "What do you think?" or "How does that work for you?" you force people into a thumbs-up or thumbs-down vote. You are forcing them to love it or hate it, nothing in between. As you've most likely experienced, most people will hate it. It's human nature to poke holes and see the challenges first. It's our fight-or-flight response trying to protect us from potential danger, aka something unusual. In that moment, you have inadvertently killed any chance for your innovative ideas to be heard, let alone gain traction from the people who matter.

As the keeper of the innovation, what do you do? You classify those very few people who gave it the up vote as the people who get it and those who voted thumbs-down as the "Yes, but-ers"— and who needs them anyway. It turns out you need them if you want to get anything done.

It's demoralizing not to have your voice heard, so let's give you the key part of the Language of Innovation tool I've been using for years with great success. It may feel like pandering, but if you change your language, you change your outcomes. I call it Open Questions.

This language change works in one-on-one meetings, large presentations, live conferences, and virtual meetings. Any time you present your thinking, whether it's just the nugget of an idea or a fully thought out solution you've been working on for months, consider your introductory technique. Let's go back to our everyday example of the high-tech water bottle. I know you just read this example, but to get the full depth of the tool, don't skip to the end. I want you to read the example in full again.

I've got this new water bottle idea totally unlike the one we sell now. This one has a built-in thumb sensor so it knows what vitamins you need and adds them to the water. It also has a temperature setting so it cools down when it's too hot and vice versa. And because it knows your thumbprint, it doesn't let anyone else open up the cap but you. *What would you do to strengthen the idea?*

Can you feel the difference? When I do this live, I can almost see the wheels turning. Instead of getting a yes or no vote, I've now engaged you. The mind doesn't like open loops, and I've just given you one to solve. How would you strengthen my idea? More drastically, instead of pushing my thinking onto you, I am inviting you along for the ride with me. When you do this, people become more open and receptive. On top of that, you've now asked them to help you make your thinking stronger, and they will. The truth is none of us has all the answers, so you need others to help complete your thinking for you. It's egotistical of any of us to think we have all the answers. Now, with the people on the other side of the table open and engaged, your voice is being heard and your ideas are getting traction.

I've found there are three winning phrases:

#1: What would you do to strengthen the idea?
#2: What does it need to include to work for you?
#3: What holes do you see and how would you fill them?

A man with a determined look on his face once rushed me as I came off stage from an innovation keynote where I shared this tool. Before I could even say hello, he launched into a question: "My boss always uses cost to shut down everyone's ideas. He always says it will cost too much and we don't have the resources. It's his idea blocker and it's hard to argue with. What do I do about people like him?"

It's easy to use cost and lack of resources to shut down ideas, even if you don't know what the price tag is. I see it happen all the time. My advice to him was simple: "For people like him who like to throw cost around like it's a weapon, I say 'How does my idea need to change to be cost-worthy?' This way, I'm not asking them *if* they'll fund it or *if* we have the resources, I'm asking them *how*. It's a very different question that usually leads to a very different answer."

As someone wise once said, "Your answers are only as good as the questions you ask." This is particularly true when it comes to having your voice and your ideas heard and valued. Getting buy-in from those who matter isn't about the idea, it's about how you communicate that idea.

Feel the Pain to See the Possibilities

Got Milk?

Do you remember that iconic advertising campaign from the 1990s? If you remember it, clearly you are a Boomer or Gen Xer, like me. If you are too young to remember all the milk moustaches on billboards across the country, take a moment to Google it. It was a marketing campaign with a simple slogan that became part of the tapestry of American culture in the '90s.

While the young adult in me has fond memories of that ad, what's more interesting is how Jon Steel and the group at the advertising agency Goodby, Silverstein & Partners came up with the slogan.[1] They did something most people in the market research world might think is a little crazy. Typically, in trying to understand the benefits of a product or service, you ask your customers to tell you what they like. You ask them questions, such as "What does ABC product do for you?" or "What value does XYZ service provide?" Makes sense, right? You want to know why they buy and, hopefully, love your product or service so you ask them directly. Except often, people can't clearly express the benefits of something, especially something like milk, which they might drink every day. It's almost too close to home. I know from years of market research that leaping directly to benefits brings out superficial answers. In my opinion, it's why a lot of marketing fails, and doesn't break through the superficial to a more meaningful level.

Jon Steel and his team clearly recognized this and decided to take a more drastic approach. They asked a group of participants to stop using milk for a week. Think about this for a second. How often do you use milk in your cereal, coffee, baking, or as a beverage? Over 80 percent of American households are drinking milk on any given day.[2]

What happened in this focus group was astounding. Suddenly, instead of the usual detached conversation, Jon and his team were faced with a group of emotional human beings, mourning the loss of their beloved milk, something they never even gave a second thought to before. Unable to use milk for a week, their morning rituals were disrupted and their go-to meals were unavailable. Talk about disrupting your daily life.

In feeling the pain of abstaining from milk, these consumers were finally able to articulate what their daily milk meant to them.

People need to feel the pain to see the possibilities. I heard a rumor once that Art Fry, the creator of the Post-it note, unable to get buy-in for his idea, gave stacks to the administrative assistants of the leaders that said no to commercializing the idea, and when they ran out the angry calls for more came flooding in.

I couldn't find a way to prove this story so I did a test in my own office. I snuck into the office early one Monday morning and removed all the Post-it notes. I took them from the supply closet, people's desks, even the conference room. I hid them all in a secret stash in my office. By noon, I could hear the grumbling, and by the end of the day all mayhem had broken loose. People were frantically searching the office like little kids who are told there's a candy stash nearby. When we reassembled for our Tuesday morning team meeting, I dumped out all the stacks of yellow onto the table. It was like a Hungry Hungry Hippo game of grab the Post-it notes. Afterward, I asked the team why they loved the sticky notes so much and almost everyone said something to the effect of "I didn't realize it, but I need them to..." By the end of the meeting, they were hugging (or protecting) their Post-it notes.

As innovators it's easy to jump immediately to the opportunity. You see how the solution is going to solve your problem. You recognize why going after a certain distribution channel is going to improve lagging sales. But the people on the other side of the table may not see it. They may need to feel the pain first.

Make them feel the lagging sales. I don't mean show them a graph. Graphs don't make you feel anything. No one walks away from a meeting and thinks, *Wow, that graph hit me right in the feels.* Paint them a picture of how that downward arrow equals more work, increased pressure, and puts you all in catch-up mode.

If you have a product prototype, make a few, give it to those people you need buy-in from, and then, when they ask for more, say no. That's when the pain kicks in.

At a primal level, we are motivated by two things: avoiding pain and seeking pleasure. Interestingly, we are more motivated to act when we are avoiding pain. Think about what drives you to action. Most of us are quick to move if we anticipate a threat to us, aka pain. That pain doesn't have to be from a tiger bite. We'll move just as fast away from psychological pain. It can be in an immediate threat to our business results, a sense of lacking in recognition, or an indicator that failure is imminent.

The next time you are presenting, don't immediately jump to list all the possibilities. Take a few minutes to steep everyone in the pain. Set the stage, and you'll discover that your audience will understand the power of the possibilities you are presenting.

What's in It for Them

We are often so busy thinking about ourselves and the impact we can have that we forget to think about others. As I've already mentioned, we are all just humans trying to innovate and be valued for those innovative contributions. The same applies for the person on the other side of the table. The next time you are pitching an idea, showing the results of an experiment, or simply trying to get buy-in to move forward on something, I want you to take a moment and ask yourself these two questions:

#1: If I were in their shoes, how would this idea impact me? Positive answers could include an opportunity to hit revenue targets and show I am looking to grow the business—I could even get promoted. Negative answers might include risking current revenue streams and facing a negative impact on the bottom line while we establish distribution—I could even get negative feedback in my performance review. Include ways that show that what you want could impact someone else on your team. This isn't an either/or exercise. Answers can, and most likely will, be positive and negative.

#2: If I were in their shoes, what are the things I'd care about most? Positive answers may include looking like an innovative leader to my boss, removing work from my plate, or being able to see my kids more. Negative answers might include being seen as impulsive, adding work to my already full plate, or spending more time on the road and, hence, less time with my family.

While question number one is the professional side, this second query covers the personal side of "What's in it for them." As we bring our whole selves to work, it's important to tackle both sides of the question.

Taking five minutes to recognize what's in it for the people you are speaking with is a simple yet powerful thing to do. It builds rapport and opens up their willingness to listen to you. We all have baggage, good and bad, we are carrying around every day. This technique ensures you are addressing that baggage so it doesn't block your brilliant innovation from getting through to decision makers.

Speak Directly to Their Everyday Innovator Style

We think of personality traits or archetypes as information about how someone speaks and acts, but they also hold the key to how they listen and engage. For example, Instinctual Experientials have a certain innovation language they not only speak but listen to. The same is true for all the Everyday Innovator styles.

If you want to bring out the innovator in those around you, above you, or beneath you on the organizational ladder, you have to speak their language. Navigating how to communicate with others in a way that speaks to them is actually easier than it sounds because it's directly related to their Everyday Innovator style. It's not about what motivates you, it's about navigating what motives them.

For instance, if you tell me, a Risk Taker Experiential, the project I'm about to work on will help me connect with others and dig into problems, I'm *mildly* in. But if you frame it as an opportunity to be bold and explore new territory, I'm *totally* in!

Different teammates have different motivators. The language that motivates each of us is different. What motivates you might not motivate others. In fact, it's more likely that what motivates you doesn't motivate others.

For years, I've studied what motivates people, specifically, to be more innovative.

I'm a Risk Taker Experiential. I'm motivated by bold opportunities and the ability to build something.

Laura, a member of our team, is a Collaborative Tweaker. Building connections with others and problem solving motivate her.

When I go to Laura with a new task, I make sure to find ways that allow her to work with others. I also go to her with sticky challenges. These challenges motivate her to dig in and figure out how to solve them. She gains a lot of satisfaction from solving these problems and also through the *process* of solving them.

Here's a recent real-world example from our team meetings:

Laura, we need to find a better way to track inquiries so we can see what we are working on and how we can track them through the process. Here's my start to it (because I'm an Experiential and need to build to see what I want), but I can't figure out how to make it work. Can you figure this out? You may want to talk to Josh and Kory about how they might approach the challenge, too.

In 24 hours, we had a tracking system up and running that we still use.

One of my business partners, who manages our digital marketing is an Instinctual Collaborative. Connecting the dots in his work and building new connections with people and information motivates him. Whenever we meet up, I'm always sure to give him a chance to flex those innovation muscles.

Specific Everyday Innovator Motivators

IQE Trigger	Collaborative	Experiential	Fluid	Futuristic	Imaginative
Motivator	Making Connections	Building Something	Creating Clarity	Future Plans	Bringing Novelty

IQE Trigger	Inquisitive	Instinctual	Risk Taker	Tweaker	
Motivator	Uncovering Things	Finding Connections	Bold Opportunities	Problem Solving	

This chart gives you an overview of what motivates different Everyday Innovator styles. It's part of understanding the Language of Innovation.

Engaging yourself. Knowing what truly motivates you can help ignite your inner motivation. As a Collaborative Fluid once told me, they used this knowledge to make sure they were working more in teams and removing some of the assumed guardrails on his work. Setting himself up for success in this way ensured that, every day, he was motivated to bring his A game. And when he wasn't feeling it (we all have those days), he went out and sought new perspectives and experiences to put himself where he thrives as a Collaborative, gathering idea points. He also took those times to find the sticky, messy projects and place himself in the center to do what he loves—as a Fluid—and find that clarity.

Set up your tasks in a way that works for you, find your motivation when it's lacking, and ignite innovation when you feel stagnant. These are the benefits of having a rich understanding of how *you* operate as an Everyday Innovator.

Engaging others. When you speak their language, you open up their ability to be innovative. It's that simple. When I work with teams, I make sure to speak not just my language but as many languages as possible to tap into the diverse group in the room. Knowing this about others gives you the power to engage each other authentically and deeply.

Set up your tasks in a way that works for you and for your team. Find the motivations so everyone brings their A game and ignites innovation when the work or the situation feels stagnant. These are the benefits of having a rich understanding of how *others* operate as Everyday Innovators.

Here are some things I've heard said around my and my clients' offices that may help you put the Language of Innovation into action.

*"I think this is a great opportunity to help the team figure out **where we should focus** and **build some new prototypes** to test out."*

—Speaking to a Fluid Experiential

*"I'm wondering if it makes more sense **to ignite some novel and fresh ideas** instead of going over the stale ones? There are probably some **not-so-obvious connections** we are missing."*

—Speaking to an Imaginative Instinctual

*"I'm struggling today. Could you help me **figure out what's going on** with this project and **what needs to happen next?**"*

—Speaking to a Tweaker Futuristic

*"I feel like my ideas are all close in. I could use your help **making them bigger and bolder.** Can **we work together** on this for an hour?"*

—Speaking to a Risk Taker Collaborative

*"Would you **dig a little deeper** on this issue and see what we are really dealing with? I think it's all there, but I'm not **connecting the dots** for some reason."*

—Speaking to an Inquisitive Instinctual

Think about where in your work you need help or need to engage the team. Write out a statement that would speak to a specific person or team's innovative side similar to the ones above. In your next interaction, use your statement and see what happens. I bet you'll find a little more leaning in. When you start intentionally connecting with people on this level, it will become second nature.

Sometimes I just walk by and smile when I hear my team tapping the diversity and innovating together. I can see the person receiving the statement light up. It's done in an authentic way that respects the value the other person brings. This also applies to team meetings and weaving in various motivators who tap everyone in the room. Simply remembering you have a room full of diverse thinkers and crafting your language in a way that engages everyone is a powerful tool that pays off dividends immediately and over time.

When You Don't Know How They Innovate

I walk into Frank's office for an early morning meeting. The moment I sit down, I notice how, on one hand, the main desk where he works day to day is almost empty—just a pad of paper and his computer. But behind him, against the wall, the credenza is filled with papers, a few prototypes I can't figure out, some duct tape, and pens of all colors. I make a mental note as we start our discussion. He tells me about his biggest frustration as a leader. In a calm and concise manner, he shares how he feels as his team really struggles with ambiguity and doesn't tend to move ideas much past the possibilities phase. He's frustrated by their lack of quality work, and they are frustrated because, no matter how hard they try, they don't seem to get it right. Everyone is frustrated. He makes statements such as "I need to know where the rubber meets the road" and "If we can navigate the situation better, we'll find the opportunities."

In Frank's office, through his language and even his hand gestures, which are precise, I suspect Frank is an Experiential Fluid. Sure enough, when he took the IQE, my suspicions were proved accurate. Seeing this helped me to understand him and his perspective and, in turn, how to bring out his Everyday Innovator style by using the Language of Innovation in our conversation.

Pay attention to the cues of the person with whom you are speaking. What language do they use? What types of crutch phrases do they tend to use? The cues are there for you. Even if you don't get it 100 percent right, you'll be more intentional in how you communicate in a way that works for that person.

At the innovation and brand strategy firm where I was VP, we had a unique challenge. Our clients loved the work we did, but as soon as the consulting work was over, we didn't have any other way for clients to engage with us. We were a one-and-done shop, hoping they would do a similar branding or new product project again. However, that didn't usually happen for at least another year. It made predicting our income tough and meant we were constantly pounding the pavement for new business. With that challenge, I tasked my team to come up with a range of new revenue streams that would help us get and keep clients.

For months, the team did research, talked to clients, and studied the industry. When the team began to share their results, they told me things like, "In theory, this will give clients a way to engage with us after the project is complete," and "XYZ competitor also does this, so we know it's proven to work." I started to yawn as they rambled on. So rude of me, right?! I couldn't help it, I was bored and not buying in to their thinking. We all left that meeting frustrated. I was frustrated because I didn't think we had anything worth pursuing, and they were frustrated because they felt their hard work wasn't valued. Both of us were right in our frustration, but it was misplaced.

I ultimately realized that what caused the breakdown wasn't the ideas but how the ideas were communicated. I'm an Experiential Risk Taker. That means I innovate in action and like to get uncomfortable and think big. By telling me "in theory," they shut down my Everyday Innovator, Experiential, which needs to experiment and test ideas. In sharing with me that the ideas were proven because others (competitors) were already doing it was in direct conflict with my Risk Taker, which wants to be bold and daring.

I bet you are wondering what they should have said. Instead of saying "in theory" or "hypothetically speaking," when you talk to an Experiential, you want to say something like, "We tested this by talking to ABC client," or, "Where the rubber meets the road in this idea is where…" Instead of sharing with me how others were already doing this idea, they should have said, "This is a stretch from where we are…," or, "While RST competitor does this, we can do it in a different and more powerful way."

It was not the team's fault. None of us realized why we were struggling, and we did eventually launch some great new revenue streams that grew our client value, but we did create an unnecessary barrier to our progress by communicating in a way that conflicted with our styles of innovation.

I wish I had known then what I know now. Of course, it should be everyone's job to be open enough to see an idea for what it's worth, but it sure helps when someone is speaking your language.

Each trigger has certain behaviors, language, and moods. It's not to say people aren't flexible in how they behave, but there are patterns that can help you navigate your communication and connection with them. As soon as you recognize what may be happening with your group, take a step back, adjust your thinking, and try a different tack.

While I hope everyone on your team and in your life invests in being their best by taking the IQE, I recognize that, like my meeting with Frank, you will often find yourself in situations where you don't know their style of innovation but need them to be open and receptive to innovative thinking. The next time you are in this situation with a group of friends, colleagues, or customers, try to figure out their Everyday Innovator styles based on the clues they give you. Then encourage them to take the IQE so you can see if you are right.

In all seriousness, why does this challenge matter? Because you will definitely be in a situation where you need the people across the table from you to move past "incremental" to "innovate." You might be seeking buy-in for a new initiative you want to test. Or maybe you'll be presenting findings from a research project or results from last Quarter's sales. Regardless of the situation, you want to tap the people in the room to be open to innovation and to contribute their innovative minds to your work. If you know what type of Everyday Innovator they are, it's easy—just be sure to communicate in their style. If you don't know, use their clues. You may not be 100 percent right, but I promise you'll be better off than if you just went through the motions and hoped for the best. You read my baby care story (page 174) and how that went for me—not well—and most likely it won't for you either. Pay attention to the cues, use their language. Following is a cheat sheet of styles and what to look for; create a fun challenge for yourself to figure out how to guide others to positive ways of thinking. This chart tells you everything you need to know about how to identify and communicate with the various unique Everyday Innovator styles.

Everyday Innovator Personality Cheat Sheet

Power Trigger	Language	Behaviors	Tone and Attitude
Collaborative	Together, we, collectively, collaborate, joint, our share, get your perspective, what are your thoughts?	Walking down the halls talking to everyone, calls a lot of meetings / gatherings, finds ways to work in teams, prefers to connect with a diverse set of people	Inclusive and welcoming
Experiential	Test it, let's see what happens, real world, trial, error, rubber meets the road, experimentation, experience, what did you find?	Often sketches out ideas, builds prototypes, works with hands and materials, activates projects before sharing or giving to others	Reality-based and grounded
Fluid	Navigate, flow, try out, test it, clarity, see how it goes, figure it out	Likes a variety in food, music, and style; either superorganized or disorganized desk	Clarifying and calm
Futuristic	Could, would, will do, envision, picture this, what if	Easily distracted, stares off into distance when thinking, maps out thinking	Opportunity and dreaming

Power Trigger	Language	Behaviors	Tone and Attitude
Imaginative	What if, possible, how about, imagine, create, build, envision, develop	Eyes-up searching imagination for new thinking, daydreaming, asks "what if" a lot	Opportunity and creative
Inquisitive	How, why, when, could it be, how about, what about, why not?	Still asking questions when everyone else is done, likes to believe but validate with their own research	Curious and questioning
Instinctual	I feel, I wonder, I believe, know this, get the sense that, a pattern of, in my gut	Hands on heart or face while thinking or talking, tends to hug or touch people's shoulders or arms when they connect, sometimes quiet to take in all the information	Heart-based and emotive
Risk Taker	I, me, daring, impact, change, disruptive, I challenge, why not?	Sees challenges as a dare, will cut you off while speaking if you get too negative, excitable	Declarative and opportunistic
Tweaker	What's working, not working, edit, evolve, shift, tweak, build	Always messing with things after others are done with them, doesn't speak in final language like "success" or "failure"	Receptive and questioning

Chapter 12

Leading Innovation & Accepting Failure

Why Failure Matters to Innovation

It would be remiss of me to write a book about innovation culture and how you can be a stronger innovator without covering the topic of failure. Failure is a natural and necessary part of innovation. Innovation thought leaders give a lot of lip service to failure, but I think most of them get it wrong and miss the big scary issue lying just underneath the surface: fear. Let's address failure and, in doing so, tackle the fear associated with it.

We've all heard the mantras around failure:

"Fail fast. Fail often."
"Love your failures."
"You can't succeed without failure."

But why? Why is failure so important to innovation and success? And why are we told to embrace failure rather than run away from it? We are often told it's because we learn the most from our mistakes. The obvious answer is that if you aren't failing, you aren't trying hard enough. You are taking the comfortable path. If you aren't failing, you aren't pushing the boundaries of what's possible. You should fail fast so you can learn and grow.

I've come to believe there is actually a deeper, more emotional reason failure is important to each of us, personally and professionally.

Failure Breaks Down Our Egos

Our egos keep us complacent, safe, and right. The ego doesn't like the prospect of innovation because it bumps up against its need to look right. You can't guarantee you are going to look smart with the inherent uncertainty that innovation includes. When you fail, your ego gets stripped away. Once the failure is out there, why not take that risk? Why not make the bold move? Why not be more innovative? You have nothing to lose after all…you've already failed.

Here are the three reasons I think the big hairy elephant we call "failure" is truly important to your personal success and to that of your team. It's also the reason it is so hard.

#1: It Opens You Up to Listening

When your ego isn't telling you that you have all the answers, you become open to other people's perspectives and ideas. You admit you don't know it all and look to others to fill the gaps in your knowledge. With new people comes fresh thinking, different perspectives, and important human connections that make your initial idea stronger.

When I was 24, I tried to launch an online fitness tracking business. Every time I ran the idea by people, they said things like, "It's too early," or, "You may want to find a partnership with a big brand that can implement it immediately," or, "I have a few ideas that may make your idea better." I didn't want to hear any of it because, of course, I knew it all. They clearly didn't see my vision, and I definitely did not need their help. My idea was brilliant on its own.

Except it wasn't, and the first attempt to launch failed. Actually, it failed in a big ball of flames that slammed to the ground. Then I had no choice but to listen. And when I did, everything changed. These people I had ignored helped me see the holes in my thinking. They gave me solutions to my biggest challenges. They steered me in the right direction.

At that time, I needed to fail to be open to their voices. Now I listen as often as I can. *Failure forces you to listen.*

#2: You Will Own Your Mistakes

What you can't run or hide from, you own. When you own your mistakes, you take accountability for them. When you take accountability, you can see your mistakes clearly. When you see your mistakes clearly, you can begin to do the real work of fixing or pivoting in new, more effective directions.

There is something freeing about removing the excuses and owning your mistakes. It allows you to take a breath, center yourself, and work through it.

Once upon a time, I had a boss who was the king of finger pointing. Nothing was his fault. Every little mistake could be traced to someone else or an external factor, obviously beyond his control. Until one day…his failure was big and public, and he was unable to avoid the inevitable. But the most amazing thing happened. Unlike past excuses that allowed him to brush off his mistakes and operate without changing, he was forced to face his epic failure head-on. The idea that bombed led to his greatest success because, for the first time, he owned his reality.

#3: You'll Get Vulnerable, Really Vulnerable

Vulnerability is tough. It requires you to be raw and open to saying "I need help" or "I don't know what I'm doing." We are so afraid of being vulnerable that we wrap ourselves in our fragile egos and pretend we have it all together. I don't know about you, but I don't have it all together. Heck, some days I don't even feel like I have some of it together.

Real innovation requires vulnerability. It requires us to take a big leap outside our comfort zones and take risks when we aren't certain of the outcomes.

When you fail, you tend to get more vulnerable because you have no choice. But it's in midst of failure where the innovation magic happens.

My mom sent me a packet of newspaper clippings from the early days of my career. They were various announcements about me taking a position as a leading executive at a global communications firm in New York City. When I reread the articles, I was transported back in time and reminded how insecure I felt. I had been offered, and accepted, a job way above my experience. I was so afraid someone would realize I had no idea what I was doing that I did my best to hide it.

I'll never forget my first big presentation to the bigwigs at the firm. I bombed so hard I was sure the people in the office across the street were shaking their heads in disappointment. Afterward, one of my bosses came into my office and said, "Tamara, it's okay to get some help in the beginning. We didn't hire you because you've already done this. We hired you because we believe you can get us further. But you'll need to admit what you don't know if you want to make that happen."

It was a game-changing moment for me. Here was my boss giving me permission to be vulnerable. I think that's some of the best advice I've ever received. However, I was only open to hearing his advice because I was in a moment of failure.

Now I have no problem pulling back the curtain, being vulnerable, and even asking for help. Failure isn't just about learning, it's about opening up.

Every day you have a choice. You can run away from failure, or you can embrace it and all the messy, uncomfortable lessons it has to offer. You can give failure lip service, or you can create a culture where listening to others, owning your mistakes, and being vulnerable is encouraged.

Making Failure Okay

In my 25 years of playing in the innovation space and partnering with Fortune 500 companies and start-ups, I've come to realize the most successful leaders say "I'm wrong" more than they say "I'm right." Truly successful leaders who seek to build an environment where failure and innovation are woven into the tapestry of their culture don't try to have all the answers. In fact, it's their willingness to recognize other perspectives and the openness to new thinking that makes them successful leaders, regardless of their professional titles. The openness is what allows them to find the most innovative answers. It's easy to fall into the trap of believing that being an innovator or in a role of leadership is about having all the answers. It turns out, the opposite is true.

Four phrases I recognize in true successful leaders are:

#1: I'm Wrong

That's a hard one to say. Most people take admitting their mistakes as a personal failure...as if being wrong makes them wrong as a person. Your ego wants to protect itself, and admitting you are wrong puts a big dent in your fragile id, the part of your unconscious mind that relates to your most basic needs and desires. But innovation requires mistakes...sometimes lots of them.

Making mistakes means you are learning and growing. It means you tried a lot, and some things worked and some didn't. Without mistakes, we wouldn't have laundry detergent or Post-it notes.

An innovator knows that "I'm wrong" is one of the most powerful phrases one can utter. In fact, it's the confident person who can admit their mistakes, learn from them, and evolve. It's the most insecure people who try to be right and hide mistakes at all costs.

If you want to be an Everyday Innovator and a leader, recognize that it's not only okay to be wrong, it's expected. If you are someone who makes statements like "Right all along" or says "I always knew it," I'd question whether you have a severe case of tunnel vision. Edison was wrong a thousand times before he figured out the lightbulb.

#2: Tell Me More about That

Years ago, I closed on the biggest innovation engagements of my young career. I was only 32, and the deal was worth a quarter of a million dollars. When I heard the client on the other end of the phone say, "We'd love to work with your company and specifically you, Tamara," I was blown away. Later, after I felt as if the client and I had a strong rapport, I braved the question, "What made you decide to go with us?"

He told me something I'll never forget:

Tamara, all the other leaders in innovation we talked to were quick to jump to solutions. They had an answer to every question we asked. We couldn't even take a breath before they jumped in. You, on the other hand, would pause and, instead of answering the question, you kept saying back to us, "Tell me more about what makes you ask that?" or "I don't yet know, but I think it's worth exploring." We got more clarity and insight in those moments than in the solutions everyone else provided. It was as if your desire to uncover the "why" for yourself helped us do the same. That's why we enthusiastically hired you.

Often, as someone looking to lead, you think you have to be the solution person. The minute someone asks a question, you expect you should jump to the answer. But what I've learned over the years is that the "why" behind the question is more powerful and more insightful than the question itself.

If you want to be a successful leader, one who ignites a culture of innovation, get into the habit of pausing and asking a question in response to your clients' questions or simply saying "tell me more." You'll be amazed at what you learn.

#3: I Don't Know

Much like "I'm wrong," "I don't know" is hard for many of us to say. Again, you are supposed to know everything, aren't you? Of course not, that's why we have teams, hire experts, and seek advice. Nobody has all the answers. What you do have is the ability to find out the answer.

I was once in a meeting with the vice presidents at a major consumer packaged goods company; there were at least 10 of us in the room discussing the direction of the brands and products they each ran, totaling over $750 million in annual sales. As we went around the room sharing, each VP gave a confident-sounding and

clear answer to why their businesses were lagging or thriving…
until Doug. Doug looked around the room and, with a clear
head and just as much confidence as everyone else, said, "I don't
know." Then he followed it up with, "We've had this crazy spike
up and down in our performance. Instead of coming up with the
answer today, we decided to take a step back and dedicate time
and resources to understanding why, so we can move forward cor-
rectly. But until we dig in, I don't know."

Wow! Can you imagine being in a room with your peers, the
people you are judged against, the people who seemingly have the
answers, and admitting "I don't know"?

What happened next was very interesting. It was as if a collec-
tive sigh of relief swept across the room. First, Jennifer, at the other
end of the table, spoke up and said, "You know, we aren't totally
sure about why our dip in the Midwest was so big."

And then Peter piped in with, "I wish we knew more." Soon,
almost everyone in the room was admitting their lack of knowledge.

Later, many of the VPs admitted to me that was the most productive meeting they'd ever had. They said it freed them up to
drop the "showboating" and focus on the work that needed to be
done—figuring out what they didn't know.

The phrase "I don't know" is vulnerable and real. It doesn't
show insecurity; in fact, quite the opposite. It shows confidence.
Confidence that it's okay not to know something; confidence in
your ability to figure it out. Doug was one of the most confident
leaders with the most innovative answers I have ever heard, and he
often said, "I don't know." And then he followed it up with how
he was going to find out. The ability to say "I don't know" and the
curiosity to find out are powerful tools in building a culture where
failure and innovation thrive.

#4: I Want to Share Something Personal...

Be professional...
Leave your personal life at home...
Don't get mushy at work...

We hear these phrases all the time. But I witnessed something that proved to me the power of being personal with people in a business environment. I had the good fortune of being the only outside keynote speaker for the annual meeting for Red Robin, the national burger and brews restaurants. It was a fantastic multiday experience that was all brought home with the final talk from the then CEO, Denny Marie Post. Instead of wrapping up the two days of business progress reports and future business presentations with more business, she got personal. She shared an incredibly personal story about resilience. You could feel the vulnerability from the stage, and you could feel the connection taking place with all 1,500 employees in the room, but not because her story was or wasn't relatable to them. Rather, by sharing something extremely personal, she built a human connection. Looking around the room, I could see the warmth, respect, and the engagement elevate with every sentence of her story.

Denny is a Collaborative Instinctual, so it makes sense that she would get personal. She innovates by connecting the dots in new and meaningful ways in those connections with people of all types and Everyday Innovator styles. I'll never forget how, after I spoke, she made a comment about how she loved having me there because she always felt that everyone contributes to innovation. She couldn't be more right!

We all have our experiences, our stories, and our baggage. It's human nature to see connection and to want to be communal, even for the most individualistic solo wolves (myself included). We want our leaders to show vulnerability and connection, too. I'm not saying leaders shouldn't get down to business, and I'm definitely not saying work is chatty time. What I'm saying is to bring your entire self to work.

Just because you're a leader doesn't mean you suddenly have to check parts of your life and personality at the office door. In fact, it's a mandate that leaders, more than anyone else in an organization, should bring their authentic self to the office. Why? Because they set the tone. If you want to motivate people to follow you to the ends of the earth, get personal with them.

Don't be afraid to put yourself out there. Leadership and innovation require vulnerability, courage, and openness.

Chapter 13

Creating a Culture of Innovation

My colleague Gail once shared a very important point with me: those who actually live the culture every day aren't the ones charged with it. They are the "grunts" doing the work. Many times, I've kicked off an innovation session with clients to hear all the right things from leadership: "We embrace a culture of innovation, where we embrace failure, recognize it doesn't happen overnight, and value input from all our employees." I leave those meetings feeling optimistic about our starting point. But, then, continuing with my innovation audit with the team, the responses I get tend to tell a different tale: "Failure is not actually accepted, leadership wants me to do as told, their innovation channels are a black hole." You get the picture. Often, what this really boils down to is great intention neither scaled nor realized. Let's bridge that gap with some proven strategies that ensure you build a culture of innovation that scales across all your teams, not just in the leadership meeting on Monday mornings.

Ditch the Presentations

There's a chasm in innovation. On one hand, the most innovative ideas look the wildest on paper, yet in the real world they are the ones we reward. Think about your favorite brand or business. Is it the one that does it like everyone else, or does it do things a little differently in a way that speaks to you?

When I ask this question in meetings, I usually get responses that include brands like Patagonia, Apple, Southwest, and Airbnb. See the pattern? How wild do you think it sounded in a conference room when someone said something like, "Let's get rid of assigned seating and just have people line up," or, "What if you rented a room at a complete stranger's house when you traveled?" These ideas probably sounded crazy to the person on the other side of the table.

Innovative ideas get killed on paper and in the conference room, where they look too wild to pursue. Yet those that leap over the chasm to reality win. Unfortunately, most die a quick and painful death before they have a chance to be tested or vetted.

To build a culture of innovation, I urge you to ditch the culture of presentation where ideas go to die and create a culture of experimentation.

One of my favorite examples of the culture of experimentation fully realized is Tough Mudder. If you've tried it, I commend you. If you haven't heard of it, Tough Mudder is an extreme sports obstacles race where the goal is not to be the fastest; the end game is teamwork and the reward is the badge value of completing the event. It was developed by Will Dean while he was a student at the Harvard Business School along with his friend Guy Livingstone, a New York lawyer. Dean submitted their idea to Harvard's yearly business plan competition, but the proposal didn't win. Why? In my opinion, their idea did not seem viable because innovative ideas look crazy on paper and at the time most competition events were solo races, like marathons and triathlons. Armed with only Facebook advertising and the power of word-of-mouth, they experimented with their crazy idea. On May 2, 2010, the first Tough Mudder challenge occurred at Bear Creek Mountain Resort in Pennsylvania...with 4,500 participants.[1]

Now they are a massive organization with events all over the world. Their followers are so loyal some of them tattoo the Tough Mudder logo after finishing, a little like bikers with Harley-Davidson ink.

My point is that the billion-dollar business didn't start with millions in investment and hundreds of events lined up. No, it started because Will and Guy took a leap over the chasm and experimented.

Creating a culture of experimentation will do two very important things. First, it will ensure you are tapping the power of all the Everyday Innovators on your team by letting them explore and pursue their ideas. They'll no longer be trapped in their heads or killed the instant they hit a slide show. Second, the ideas and solutions you decide to pursue will be battle tested. How many times have you seen something launched directly from the conference room succeed? It doesn't happen. Usually, the conference-room initiative crashes and burns in a massive fireball of disappointment. A culture of experimentation helps you truly determine the worth of your thinking. It's real-world feedback every step of the way. You'll be able to adjust and optimize with every experiment. You'll discover new opportunities, gaps you didn't see, ways to improve—by ditching the presentation.

Creating a culture of experimentation takes teams out of the mind-set that presentations and reports are milestones that determine success and recognizes that the action and data in the experimentation are your true gauges of success. Experimentations can be small, building over time. A rough prototype made of duct tape and a box from the grocery store, a mock one-page marketing sheet to show a client, a dark corner of the office where you can implement your solution with one person to see what happens could be all you need.

Build experiments into your processes. Encourage people around you to test their ideas before a presentation. At some point, you will need to share your idea with the people who will sign off on it, but imagine how much more persuasive your thinking will be when you show them real-world feedback and results, not just an idea with some hypothetical data.

As Mike Dubin, the founder of Dollar Shave Club, once said to me on Inside LaunchStreet, "It sounded like a good idea in theory, but you never know until you actually put it on the market and see what the take is."

The market can be anyone—from your employees to your leadership to your customers.

Embrace the J-Curve

Wouldn't it be great if every time we decided to be innovative everything went our way? The minute we pivot, everything falls into place. Every step works, and we get high fives and pats on the back from everyone in the office. Sadly, isn't that our expectation when we innovate? It's like a straight line up from the starting point of A to skyrocket success all along the way.

The truth looks nothing like a progression, does it? In fact, it looks more like a J-curve, dipping down, and then working its way back up.

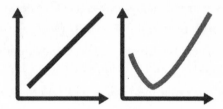

The phases of the J-curve are as follows:

First, there's the starting point. You've made the decision to implement the new process or go after that new market opportunity. You and the team, maybe even the organization, made the decision because you know it's the right thing to do. The energy is buzzing with possibilities. Everyone is on board, or so it seems.

Then the big dig in the J-curve happens. Some things worked better than expected, some did not. Often, things don't go quite as planned. If you launched a new process, perhaps you now have to duplicate your efforts while the many unanticipated kinks are worked out. Or if you've gone after a new market opportunity, it could turn out the path to entry is going to be a lot more challenging than expected. This is where the doubters and the naysayers loudly come out of the woodwork.

"I knew it would never work."
"We should shut it down before it gets worse."
"All this is doing is creating more work."
"This isn't worth the effort."

And when they take over, you begin to second-guess your decisions, doubt your own judgments, and stop seeing the light at the end of the tunnel. This phase seems dark and long.

If you aren't prepared for the J-curve of innovation, the dip is where things could get shut down. Anthony of Footers Catering, mentioned in Create the Ultimate Team-mance (page 160), shared with me that when his client-facing team decided to implement a new order processing system, the bottom of the J-curve hit them hard. Everyone was doing double the work, implementing order details on the old and new systems to ensure no data was lost. They discovered a few gaps that delayed everyone's processing and created confusion. Worst of all, the people who were comfortable with the old system began to question the entire decision, making everyone doubt their judgment.

But Anthony knew this was coming and had prepared for it. Before they did anything, he sat his team down and explained the J-curve journey they were about to go through. In doing so, he prepared his team for the fact that this wasn't going to be a straight shot to success; up next would be not just bumps but a big dip. In doing so, Anthony set his team up to handle the challenges they were about to face and not lose hope that this shift would ultimately benefit the team. And it worked. The team is now well past the dip and on the upswing portion of the J-curve, reaping the benefits of their foresight and patience.

Being aware and prepared for the realities of the J-curve is a key element to building a culture of innovation. If everything dies at the bottom of the curve, there's no incentive for your team to innovate. Why bother? It's all going to end up in the idea graveyard anyway. The only way to avoid this naysaying is to set the journey and the expectations upfront. If you are leading a team, let them know that the J-curve is coming—it's a natural and expected part of the process. In fact, the dip is a great place to keep innovating as you discover what does and doesn't work.

If you are working on an initiative and need the support of either those you work for or with on a cross-functional team, the same applies. Let them know about the J-curve up front.

Reward Behaviors, Not Outcomes

When I walk into our clients' offices, I usually see one of two scenarios:

Scenario One: Yolanda just implemented that new internal communications software for the company. Leadership wasn't sure if it would work, but it turns out communication and productivity are improving. The team is so excited that Yolanda is being rewarded with drinks and a congrats cake on Friday! When you see Yolanda in the hallway, applaud her as she walks by.

Or...

Scenario Two: Lowell went after a big opportunity in the marketplace that he thought would bring in new clients. It didn't work, and the initiative is shut down. Lowell is brought into his boss's office, where he and his boss labor over the mistakes Lowell made. At the end of a painful meeting, Lowell is told the company embraces failure, *but*...how about we wrap what happened in a pretty bow, put it on the failure shelf, and never speak of it again? In fact, Lowell is put on some smaller project so he can recover from this tragedy. If you see Lowell in the hallways, don't say a word.

It's like playing Russian roulette at work. If your team's only two outcomes for being innovative are cake on Friday or the failure shelf, how likely do you think they are to innovate? Not likely at all. In fact, the effect is negative.

If you want to build an authentic culture of innovation, reward behaviors, not outcomes. Of course you should reward a big win or a positive financial impact someone had on the bottom line, but don't ignore the behaviors that got you to those outcomes. You need lots of those behaviors to get to the positive, productive outcomes.

When I was VP of the innovation firm, I used to put the call out for suggestions—help in solving sticky client challenges, ways to improve our culture internally—for whatever I was working on that week when I felt stuck. I'd send out the email in the morning, and by the end of the day I'd have a small stack of sticky notes on my desk. I knew my team well enough to expect some of them would respond before I could blink an eye.

The interesting piece turned out to be that I was getting responses from the same set of people. While their input mattered greatly, I wanted everyone's input. One day, I got clever. Before I came to work to send one of my "request for suggestions" emails, I went to Starbucks and got a stack of five-dollar gift cards. After the initial stack of suggestions came in, I made my move. I went around the office and very publicly and loudly praised them for taking the time to provide their suggestions and passed out Starbucks cards to those who responded. I made it clear I hadn't read what they wrote yet, but I was thankful they took the time to provide their innovative thinking to my challenge. I probably sounded like I was yelling, but I wanted to make sure everyone in the office saw that I noticed and appreciated the effort. By the end of that day, I had more suggestions to go through. I needed a lot more Starbucks gift cards if this was going to continue.

Do you see what happened? In rewarding the behavior I wanted, I got more of it. More suggestions, more speaking up, and more ideas circulated around the office. Behavior creates culture.

Ray Dalio, the founder of Bridgewater Associates, one of the most successful investment firms of all times, in his book *Principles* shares how he discovered that being surrounded by yes-men was the downfall of his first company. He goes on to explain how he hires people who will disagree with him because he recognizes that counter behavior is good for the bottom line.[2]

Every team is different. Decide which behaviors you want to see more of and reward them. At my company, LaunchStreet, I reward people for doing small, no-risk experiments for their ideas because I know that helps us grow. Like Ray Dalio, I reward people who are willing to take the risk and disagree with me or anyone else on the team. I know that constructive conflict (more on that later; see page 217) makes our ideas and our decisions stronger. I reward people for living their Everyday Innovator style. If an Inquisitive on my team asks three more questions, even when I think I know the answers, I reward them. When a Risk Taker speaks up, even when the sentiment in the room is going in the other direction, I reward them.

Over the years, I've collected a list of some of the behaviors that ignite innovation. Use them as a springboard to build your own list. What is important here is that you don't let this happen by chance. Systematize rewarding behaviors. Make it a leadership mandate, create a recognition board—whatever it takes to ensure this doesn't just happen once a quarter.

I hope this list will help you think about and implement behavior rewards that matter to you, your team, and your organization. I suggest starting by choosing or creating three that you think are in line with your values. The list includes:

- Taking calculated risks
- Asking questions that challenge assumptions or decisions
- Disagreeing with leadership or the team
- Submitting suggestions or ideas
- Collaborating with others to accomplish goals
- Providing help or support to someone when it doesn't directly benefit them
- Going above and beyond in their work
- Going the extra mile for a client/customer
- Bringing up innovative solutions in meetings
- Working to get ahead of a challenge or roadblock
- Being brutally honest when it's hard to do
- Bringing new opportunities to the team
- Having a great attitude during challenging times/moments

Complete Innovation Loop

While I was speaking to a group of business leaders about creating innovation loops, a woman raised her hand, waving like crazy. Before I could acknowledge her, she started to speak. She asked me, and the group, "I have a suggestion box but no one ever uses it, so what do I do?"

Before continuing with the group, I asked her, "Do you read the suggestions from your employees?"

She responded, "When I have a chance, and, frankly, most of them are stupid so I throw them away."

While it took tremendous willpower not to laugh at the obvious pitfalls in her response, I'm glad she asked the question. I think it highlights the challenge many organizations and leaders have when it comes to gathering ideas and asking everyone to participate in innovation. It's a one-way system. In essence, you as the employee submit an idea that goes into the black hole. Who knows where it goes or what happens to it. Maybe leadership looks at it, maybe they don't. Who knows and, frankly, after a while, who cares. That one-way system most organizations have is not only a waste of time, it's also demoralizing to the team. If you have this at your office, I bet you've discovered that the quantity and quality of input diminishes over time. People begin to feel disconnected from the process and lack a sense of contribution. It doesn't matter if this is an actual box with sticky notes or a high-tech system you can log in to, nobody wants to participate in a one-way black hole of "who knows what happens next." No thanks, I'll just keep my innovative ideas to myself.

As I shared with this woman at my keynote, "If you want innovation to be everybody's business, you've got to create a system with a continuous cycle that completes a loop. Merely asking for input isn't enough." I went on to explain that a complete loop that ignites innovation across your teams involves four steps:

1: Open Up for Innovation Submissions

This can be in the form of asking a specific question, requesting feedback, or simply being open for any and all ideas. Whatever you are open for, the request must be clear and repeated. Telling your team once isn't enough. It must be woven into conversation, meetings, emails, and online bulletin boards. And people must be rewarded for taking the time to provide their input. Whatever it takes to keep it front and center in people's minds. One of my clients has a link in her signature to an open-ended survey that allows her team to submit ideas any time they choose to. As you read in Reward Behaviors, Not Outcomes (page 210), I regularly give out gift cards to people for their submissions, regardless of the content.

#2: Actively Review All Submissions

This means to dedicate time and focus to actually going through all the submissions, not just the ones from your favorite people, not just once a quarter, not looking for a specific solution. Actively review any and all submissions.

#3: Choose Submissions to Pursue

The reality is you can't move forward with every idea: some because it's the wrong time, some because they need to be fleshed out, and some may have flaws that require them to be shelved. That is perfectly fine. One of my clients has a committee that reviews every submission, maybe even goes back to ask questions of the person who submitted the idea, and then, if there are any, chooses a few ideas to move forward with. Sometimes they shelve them all; sometimes they move forward with several.

#4: Communicate Back to the Team

This is where the rubber meets the road, yet it's where most innovation efforts fail. A client of mine fully understands how important this part is so they assign each member of the leadership committee a set of ideas to own. This means reporting back to each person behind the idea on the progress. Sometimes it's how they might move forward, and sometimes it's why the idea isn't going to be pursued at this time. Is it time consuming? Yes, most definitely. But it's also very well worth it. You don't always have to do this one on one, but I do recommend finding a way to report back to everyone where you are headed and why. The "why" is one of the most important parts.

Maslow's hierarchy of needs shows us that we all crave a sense of belonging and value. Here's the fundamental truth I've discovered about making innovation everybody's business:

People Don't Need to Be Right, They Need to Be Heard

When people feel heard, they feel valued. In creating a complete innovation loop, you'll discover that it feeds on itself. As more people participate, that means more ideas, and in the increased quantity of ideas will be some gems worth pursuing. Then when you report back to the team on what you learned and what you are going to do next, people feel like their contributions matter, so they continue to participate—and the loop continues with increased engagement.

Allow for Constructive Conflict

We were in a swanky loft in New York City with a group of clients from a major beverage company. This was the brand team's strategic off-site, and we thought taking them to a cool spot out of their offices for the day and getting them an expert facilitator would help them expand their thinking. We were right *and* wrong. We had a lot of juicy topics to discuss and we knew going in there was probably going to be some heated debate throughout the day.

The facilitator had chairs set up in a large circle because he felt sitting this way was less threatening and would remove hierarchy. The facilitator started by explaining the rules of the day. If we wanted to disagree with someone, instead of saying "I disagree" we would say "I have a clarifying question." Instead of saying "No" to anything, we'd say "I might consider." And the one that became the favorite of the day, instead of saying "Yes but," we'd say "Yes and." The point was to build on, not debate, each other's thinking. He explained that if we defused the tension, we'd be able to have a civil and robust conversation.

As you can probably guess, the day was a shit show. His facilitation totally squelched our ability to have an honest conversation. No one said what they really thought. The incessant "Yes and" meant we never got into any real depth in our conversations. We became a bunch of agreeable bobbleheads. When it was over, all we had was a bunch of watered-down ideas that came from a place of false consensus.

We were all smiles and handshakes until dinner that night. One by one, the rumblings started. A few side conversations here and there, some snarky comments over salads. It became clear to me that the agreeable nature of the day did not serve us. I was already disappointed with the ideas of the day, and now I could tell there was another side effect: an unsatisfied team of people. I knew very clearly by dessert time this meeting had been a total waste of time.

While not his intent, the facilitator taught me a valuable lesson: there is value in conflict. Great innovation happens in the tension, the push and pull of ideas. That's how ideas are tested and strengthened. And conflict gives people the opportunity to speak their minds, especially when they disagree.

When it comes to innovation, we're told a myth that you need to surround yourself with people who love your ideas. You're told you should be one of those "Yes and" people. You're told you should ignore those who poke holes. They're just negative "Yes but" people who don't get it.

However, the truth paints a very different picture. What we actually want to do is to create a space for constructive conflict. When you create constructive conflict, you create tension. Great innovation comes out of that tension among ideas, disagreement, and conflict. I'm not saying you should start yelling at one another. That's not constructive and doesn't feel very good for anyone. I am suggesting that encouraging and seeking debate is highly valuable. Prod the "Yes but-ers" to find the holes in your thinking and ask them to help you fill them. This will result in more valuable lasting ideas.

If you're looking for some constructive conflict, find the person you know will have a different perspective and say to them, "Hey, I'm hoping you can find the faults in my thinking and frame up a better solution."

The next time you're in a meeting, let yourself and the team know they have permission to disagree with you. You may say something like, "I encourage you to debate or disagree should you feel differently. The key is to remember that we're debating ideas, not each other."

When you hold your next brainstorming session, call on people by saying something like, "Hey, Kris, as a Futuristic Experiential you probably see this a little differently..." or, "Horace, as a Tweaker Instinctual, I bet you have a unique perspective we aren't considering."

You have this incredible built-in mechanism for debate, a group of diverse innovators. But as in the story above, most of us are trained to not make waves and to always find the positive. You can be positive and still have a robust and constructive debate.

There's this great scene in the zombie movie *World War Z* with Brad Pitt where he's talking to an Israeli leader about how they were wise enough to build a wall to keep out the impending zombie apocalypse when everyone else across the globe was sure it wasn't going to happen and was hence caught off guard. The Israeli leader goes on to share the tenth man strategy. The tenth man strategy is what you do when everyone in the room agrees. You assign one person, the tenth man, to prove everyone wrong. Their sole job is to find the holes and create debate.

Seek out constructive conflict and you'll create bulletproof (and zombie-proof) ideas that have been stretched, poked, and strengthened.

PART IV:
SUSTAINING INNOVATION

Chapter 14

Innovator Experiments

I call the content in this chapter "experiments" because the brain reacts to experiments differently than it does to activities, tasks, or exercises. You go into an activity, task, or exercise already resisting having to do it. The brain associates hard work with worries about how you'll perform. An experiment, on the other hand, is testing the waters, giving something a try. Your brain looks at an experiment and says, "Oh, okay, let's see how this goes."

With that, the experiments in this section will work for individuals and for teams. Each of these experiments works for all the Everyday Innovator styles because they adjust to how you do them. If you are an Inquisitive Instinctual, the lens you wear and the words you choose will be different from those of a Collaborative Risk Taker. That just adds to the depth and breadth of each of the experiments. They are part of helping you continue to unlock innovation in your day-to-day work and daily life.

It was January and that meant goal setting. This was the year of going big, so I created some BHAG (big hairy audacious goals) for my business and life. It included hitting five million in revenue (even though I was only in the six figures at the time) and being a size six (even though I was a size 14 when I woke up on New Year's Day). I put my goals on sticky notes on my bathroom mirror, my desk, and my car dashboard. Every time I looked at a sticky note, I would say it out loud. Yet every time I said them, something on the inside gnawed at me. It was this quiet voice telling me this was all BS. I tried to ignore the voice—you know, "fake it till you make it"—but it wouldn't go away. No matter how hard I tried, there was this battle between my conscious and unconscious mind. Needless to say, neither of my goals came to fruition that year and I swore off goal-setting forever.

My goals didn't work because my brain didn't believe them. My brain is back there going *BS, lady, not even close.* So no matter how many times I recited my goals, I was just fighting my own beliefs. You (and your team) are always fighting your own beliefs, and you need to train your brain to break this pattern.

What I've discovered over the years is that you can maneuver around the barriers in your brain and unlock your innovative mind with ease and speed. When I discovered how to train my brain to work with me instead of against me, I plowed through goals like my kids do candy at the movie theater. These exercises are going to ensure your innovative mind is always open for business. I want to ensure that as you unlock your innovation superpowers, you are not hitting unnecessary barriers, specifically old beliefs and habits. They'll try to pull you back into old ways of doing things and keep you looking into the past instead of focusing on the future.

While these exercises are written for the individual, they can be applied to teams as well.

Taming the Lizard Brain

Fear, procrastination, self-doubt, defensiveness, playing it safe— that's how the lizard brain presents itself in your life. In my head, it's the voice telling me, *Slow your roll, girl* or *Don't say that, it's too risky*. It's the primitive part of your brain that wants to keep you safe and comfortable. It reacts quickly, controlling what information makes it past the lizard den of your mind to your higher thinking functions. You can probably feel your lizard brain as the push/pull of resistance in your mind.

Imagine being in a very important meeting. This is your chance to shine in front of the bigwigs. You present and pause for questions, nervous for what's to come. The bigwig at the other end of the table clears her throat and asks a really tough question, dripping with sarcasm. It's not one you had covered in your prep. What happens? Your body heats up a little; you can feel your heart racing, and in that moment it's as if your brain turns into scrambled eggs and you forget all the research you did supporting your thinking. That's the lizard brain taking over, flooding your brain with hormones that block your ability to think clearly. It's your fight-or-flight mechanism telling you to run away from danger. In the caveman days, your ability to detect fear without having to take the time to fully process every element of your surrounding was key to survival. In the modern world, where most of your threats are in the boardroom and not in the bushes, it tends to play tricks on you and put you into fight-or-flight mode unnecessarily.

It's the reason you keep putting off that new business call that may lead to a big opportunity. If you don't go after it, you stay safe. You failed in a small way. If you do call and they say no, you may fail big. You also may win big, but the lizard brain is more concerned with avoiding the pain of uncertainty than the pleasure of winning big.

Or have you ever had that experience where you say something you think is relatively innocuous to someone and they get defensive? I was giving one of my employees feedback on some marketing materials they created. Overall, I liked the direction they were headed and I had a few suggestions I thought would enhance the results of the marketing campaign. I wasn't two minutes in when his defensive stance took over. He started speaking in a higher pitch, defending his decisions, not even taking a breath to let me put in a word. I sat back and watched his monologue for at least 10 minutes. Finally, he took a breath, looked at me, and said, "I'm so sorry, I have no idea where that all came from!"

"I know," I said. "That was your lizard brain freaking out before you had a chance to think."

> *"The lizard brain is hungry, scared, and angry. The lizard brain is the reason you are afraid, the reason you don't do all the art you can, the reason you don't ship when you can. The lizard brain is the source of the resistance."*

—Seth Godin

The lizard brain becomes the negative chatter in your mind, holding down your ability to innovate. Except in this case, the lizard brain is the reason that, even when you know something is right, you still keep quiet.

As T. Sebastian wrote in his book *If You Have Buttons… You're a Robot: A Concise Guide to Taming Your Lizard Brain*:

When we are listening to and obeying the dictates of our programming, it's like being in a cage. Your perceptions are constantly telling you to behave certain ways. These behavioral commands are not necessarily in your best interest. And they may not even be close to what you actually want to do. These compulsive urges are mostly at odds with the creative and adventurous inside.

What the lizard brain wants and what the world demands of you are at odds. The lizard brain wants safety and consistency. You need to be innovative and adaptable. The lizard brain wants to see things as black and white, right or wrong. You need to be able to see the nuances and the patterns of the world. The lizard brain likes the familiarity of business as usual. You need to step out and find new paths and mountains to conquer.

The bad news is that the lizard brain will never go away. The good news is that the lizard brain can be tamed. In taming the lizard brain, you'll be able to unleash your full potential into the world instead of keeping it hidden inside you. I've found there are three very simple ways to tame this primitive brain function we are stuck with.

Give It a Name: I'd like to introduce you to Bernard. Bernard is a waif of a human-animal hybrid. He's slumped over, lacking in any muscle, has a horrible comb-over, and his glasses are always falling off his nose. Bernard is my lizard brain.

Giving my lizard a persona has helped me tame him because, to me, he's real and tangible. He's someone I can talk back to, shut down, and wave off. Give your lizard brain a persona you can boss around. It may sound silly, but it works. I also find that making

him weak in stature and demeanor makes me less likely to take
his advice in the first place. Half the time, when I feel him coming
on with that flutter in my heartbeat or rush of negative emotion, I
simply say, *Not today, Bernard*, and he goes away.

Question It: When Bernard is doing his thing and I'm having a
lizard brain reaction, I like to stop and ask myself (and Bernard)
some simple questions:

Wow, where is this coming from?
Why did that make me so angry/hurt/sad, etc.?
Is this truly reality or am I making things up in my mind?
Hey, Bernard, why are you so scared?
Why did I back down and not share my innovative ideas?

In asking myself a few key questions, I force myself to identify
with my emotion and response and deal with it. It only takes a few
seconds, which is just enough time to put my lizard brain in check.
I kick my more rational side into gear with a few key questions.

Three Breaths: In, out, in, out, in, out. Sometimes that's all it takes
to quiet the lizard brain. As mentioned above, the lizard brain is
impulsive and compulsive. It moves quickly so the rest of your
innovative mind can't react. What I think is sometimes funny
about the lizard brain's impulsive and compulsive nature is that
you can almost feel it happening. It's like watching a slow-motion
movie of words coming out of your mouth. While the words
are happening, the brain is yelling, *Doooooonnnnnnnn'ttttttt
Dddddddoooooooooo iiiiiiiiittttttttt!* Yet you still do.

I was having an argument with my dad. It was the usual father/
daughter debate about life choices. He said something about a few
of my life choices that sent Bernard into full charge, both arms
swinging punches into the air. I replied with a comment about

his obviously not so great parenting, if that's the kind of daughter he raised. As I was saying it, I knew it was the wrong thing to say. But in that moment, Bernard was in control and I couldn't stop. Then *my father's* lizard brain took over, and we were having a full-on lizard fight—one reptilian brain against the other. Darn lizards!

My dad and I have a wonderful relationship; he's my rock and the person I admire most in this world for his big dreams and bravery in going after them. Even between us, though, the lizards got the better of us in that moment. Looking back, I laugh at how ridiculous we both must have sounded to my sister and mom as they witnessed our verbal sparring.

I've learned that, if I feel Bernard winding up in any way, whether it's trying to get me to procrastinate, respond emotionally, or get defensive, I stop and take three breaths. That gives Bernard a chance to calm down and my whole brain a chance to think before I respond. It only takes three breaths.

Before I started taking my three breaths, I would worry that it would feel like awkward silence, but really, three seconds isn't that long. And if you are concerned about the other person, just say, "Give me a second to think about it." Buy yourself some time. With three deep breaths, you'll feel the difference.

One of my favorite tricks for buying time is to respond to a question with a question. Recall the story I shared above about a tough question you didn't expect hurtled at you. In a situation like that, when I feel the lizard brain kicking in and I know I need to give myself a few breaths, I might respond to their question with a question such as; "Interesting question, what makes you ask that?" Or "Tell me more about what makes you think that."

Two things happen here. First, it gives me a chance to flick Bernard off my shoulder and get to my rational and innovative brain. Second, I usually learn more about what the other person is actually seeking to understand. It's a double win because now I'm calm and innovative, and I'm getting to the heart of what they really care about. Bam!

Overcoming Confirmation Bias

There's growing disparity between the volume of information we take in every day and our mind's ability to consume that information. We are inundated with information every moment of every day.

Take a moment to look around you. Unless you are in a secluded cabin in the mountains with no Wi-fi, you are surrounded by the noise of the world. With mobile phones, digital media, and constant chatter, that noise is getting busier and louder. You simply can't take it all in.

Many researchers believe this information overload era we live in is what's contributing to our short attention spans. A study by Microsoft and a study done in Canada both found that the average attention span has dropped from 12 seconds to eight seconds.[1] Try counting to eight. Like me, did you get distracted before you got to six? Eight seconds is a short amount of time and yet even that is difficult.

Zach First, an Instinctual Risk Taker and the executive director of the Drucker Institute, the brainchild of the wildly insightful management guru Peter Drucker, summed it up well when I interviewed him on episode 1755 of *Inside LaunchStreet*. He talked about a phrase that Doris Drucker, Peter Drucker's wife, used to say: "information obesity." He went on to explain that information is like calories; we are taking too much in. Like food, we need to find ways to restrict our caloric, or information, intake. And, as you well know, that overload is only going to get worse...so watch your waistline.

The combination of an overload of stimulus and a short attention span means your brain has to work hard to find shortcuts. Hence, it works to filter out what's worth paying attention to and what's acceptable to ignore. It does this through an incredible filter called the reticular activating system (RAS).

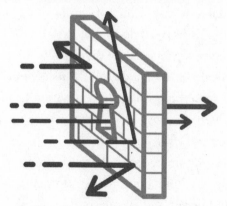

The RAS filters out what's not relevant to you and lets in what is.[2] It explains why, in a crowded room, you can tune out the chatter and then immediately perk up when someone says your name. Second, your brain looks for what's changed or is out of place. For example, it's why you get that funny feeling that something isn't right when you walk into your home after a long day at work. You didn't consciously notice that the dishwasher has leaked water over the floor, but your RAS noticed it, and now your conscious mind needs to take a second to catch up and find what's out of place. You scan the room, and there it is: soapy water all over the floor.

The RAS has a very interesting role when it comes to your ability to innovate. It actively tries to match your outside world (your environment) with your inside world (your thoughts and beliefs). This is both a blessing in the sense of keeping out the massive amounts of information we can't handle and a curse in the sense it also means we filter differing perspectives and opinions. As we've learned, those elements are essential for innovation.

The proof is in our habits. We tend to watch TV and news shows that validate our opinions; we seek out people who agree with us. We wave off people who disagree with us, or even ignore them altogether. We scroll Facebook for the posts we like, aka those that match our sense of humor, our hobbies, our views of the world. Don't feel bad; we all do it. The RAS ensures that much of the time we don't even register the differing view.

Your brain's desire to match your outside and inside worlds translates into something called "confirmation bias," *the tendency to search for, interpret, favor, and recall information in a way that affirms one's prior beliefs or hypotheses.*

Some call it cognitive poison because it deeply hinders your ability to innovate. Your brain seeks information that confirms your preexisting beliefs and ignores opinions and data that don't. The tricky part is that it's so embedded in the brain and in your behaviors that, most of the time, you don't know you're doing it.

As Richard Gregory, a perceptual psychologist in Britain stated, "This acceptance by the brain of the most probable answer makes it difficult, perhaps somewhat impossible, to see very unusual objects."[3]

In our case, unusual objects are anything different, unique, or innovative. In essence, in an effort to be efficient, your brain is seeking what it already knows, what already fits patterns you've experienced.

This may hinder your ability to spot an opportunity, find that innovative solution, or see the brilliance in someone else's wacky thinking.

But there are several ways to train your brain to overcome confirmation bias and not let it hinder your innovation efforts.

#1: Play Your Own Devil's Advocate

Intentionally try to state the opposite or argue with your own thinking. It will force you to think from a different perspective. Ask someone for an opposing opinion. Or maybe you know they are coming from a vantage point different from yours. We tend to seek out people who are similar to us. There's a reason that the phrase "birds of a feather" exists. But stepping out of the comfortable zone of "people like me" will open up whole new worlds. You'll learn more about why this is so important and how to do this in Chapter 9, Building High-Performance Teams, on team innovation. I think it's one of the reasons traveling abroad is such a powerful experience for most people. You begin to see that other types of people, ideas, and perspectives exist in the world and are valid. A great way to do this is to find someone who thinks drastically differently from you. Perhaps one of their power triggers is your dormant trigger. As an example, Jane Doe's dormant trigger is Experiential, so I would suggest she might find someone who's Everyday Innovator style includes Experiential as a power trigger.

#2: Pretend You Are Walking in Someone Else's Shoes

Imagine walking in the shoes of someone who exemplifies a completely different perspective: a boss, a customer, a competitor, someone with different political perspectives than you, or a different Everyday Innovator style. Whoever it is, debate from their point of view. This is one of my favorite exercises, and I encourage you to do it from as many perspectives as possible. Really think about their world, their experiences, their needs and desires. This will force you out of your shoes and into theirs.

> *If I were an Inquisitive, what questions would I ask to challenge my assumptions?*
> *If I were a Risk Taker, how would I try to stretch this idea until it feels uncomfortable?*
> *If I were an Imaginative, how would I take all the possibilities off the table to create something totally new?*

#3: Ask Yourself What Else Could Be True

It sounds simplistic, but we often forget that our version of reality isn't the only one. Stop and think about other "truths" or "facts" for a moment. You'll be surprised how many alternate truths you'll discover.

#4: Actively Take In Alternative Perspectives

When I'm staying in hotels for work travel, one of my favorite things to do is bounce back and forth between CNN and Fox News. It's not because I'm a news junky; quite the opposite. It's because I like to see how the different sources are reporting on the same issues. Maybe there's a perspective I didn't consider. Perhaps seeing both sides will help me build a more informed opinion of my own. Mostly, it forces me out of just nodding my head in agreement and makes me think about my own thoughts. It's a powerful thing.

When you break through your own confirmation bias, you'll be more open to seeking out the opinions of others, especially those who don't innovate the way you do. As an Inquisitive Futuristic, you'll be more open to input from an Imaginative Instinctual or a Risk Taker Fluid.

It's important to recognize unconscious bias exists and seek to break down its unconscious walls. In breaking down those walls, you'll discover innovation that might have been there all along.

The Walmart Experiment

After an illustrious career as a senior marketing executive in the consumer goods and alcohol industry, Bill Weintraub moved on to teach marketing and advertising at the University of Colorado in Boulder. While having lunch with him one day, he shared with me his frustration with his students. While they are very intelligent, they have a myopic view of the world, he said. They can't see past their own experiences. They have confirmation bias to the extreme. Bill relayed to me how they were discussing a project to create a mock marketing plan for a food product; however, the students could not grasp why everyone didn't buy fresh, certified organic food all the time. This was their only experience with food, and it couldn't be that expensive, right?! They couldn't fathom why someone would shop at Walmart and stock up on frozen food and processed snacks. He was struggling to find an exercise that would help them break their confirmation bias. And in this case, their confirmation bias was hindering their ability to be good business marketers. Actually, it hinders all of us, regardless of our role.

I felt his frustration, so I said to him, "How about making one of their projects going to Walmart and talking to people about what's in their grocery carts. I bet they'll find it eye-opening." Sure enough, semester after semester, students from his class make their way to Walmart and step into someone else's shoes. In fact, one student's experience with this project was so profound that he joined the Peace Corps and is now traveling the world. Overall, students began to recognize there are other realities for individuals in the world, other ways of thinking and acting. The Walmart experiment taught these kids to break down their confirmation bias, not just in class but across many aspects of their schooling and lives.

Creating Open Loops

I forgot to send Sally an email with directions to our meeting location.

What happened to that colleague of mine who didn't show up for work on Monday?

We never made a decision about where to launch our next product.

I forgot to put the laundry in the dryer.

I need to sign my kiddo up for the cross-country team before they close registration.

Do questions like these pop into your mind at the most random times? Your brain doesn't like open loops. It's constantly looking for closure on those things you have left unresolved in your life. It wants to figure out how to send Sally a quick email or find a time to put laundry in the dryer. Often, the open loops in your mind take up space and energy without you even realizing it. This section isn't about being more productive. For that, you should look into the methods introduced in David Allen's book *Getting Things Done: The Art of Stress-Free Productivity.*

For our purposes, instead of trying to close loops, you are going to use your brain's need to resolve open loops to your advantage.[4] You are going to use open loops to tap innovation. Instead of having your brain spin on unresolved decisions and tasks (you should just go do it), you're going to have your brain spinning on how to innovate and solve big challenges. You'll use the power of "how to" questions to tap your Everyday Innovator style to its fullest.

How do I think differently about _____?

What would it take to create a drastically different outcome for _____?

How do I turn _____ into an opportunity?

How do I bring more innovation and value to _____?

Go ahead and send off that email and finish those dishes so you can create open loops that serve you. You'll find you have more "aha" moments every day as your brain works hard to accomplish those unresolved questions you placed in your mind. We'll have your brain spinning with innovation, not procrastination.

Innovate, Then Analyze

"Your brain can't innovate and analyze at the same time."—Scott Halford, neuroscience champion

We gathered in the conference room to brainstorm new product ideas for our beauty client. None of us had the time to generate ideas beforehand, so we needed this time to pull some ideas out of the hat before our client meeting at the end of the week. We gathered our market research, had a robust conversation about the needs of our target audience, and then started throwing ideas out there. I'd throw an idea out and then find myself judging its worth to the group. Crystal would throw out an idea and then nitpick its merit. Loreli jumped in with a few ideas and then asked to scratch one off because he decided he didn't like it even as he said it.

This went on for three hours. The ideas seemed to get more incremental as the time went on. At the end of the day, we had nothing but frustration; the meeting fell flat. I went back to my office, slammed my papers down on my desk, and slumped in my chair. I couldn't figure out why the meeting turned out to be so worthless. I jumped online looking for a warm-up exercise or innovation tool kit that held the magical key to turning our meetings around. We were running out of time and I needed to get this right if I wanted to avoid egg on my face. Something about how I was running the meetings wasn't working, so I asked a colleague to take over. Maybe a change of facilitation would be all it takes to turn this sinking ship around. The next day, we assembled, ready for more of the same. But my colleague Cliff had something else in mind. He started out by saying, "We only have three hours, so we are going to spend the first two innovating, and then in the last hour we'll judge and filter down our ideas." Brilliant! For two hours, we innovated our hearts out, knowing we would have a chance to judge and critique later. By the end of this brainstorm session, we had a range of ideas we knew the client would love. I gave the team, and especially Cliff, a high five before leaving the office.

Cliff understood something I didn't. He understood that you can't innovate and analyze at the same time. Doing so shuts down the innovative mind. He knew that to achieve our objectives, he needed to do two things:

#1: Separate the Activities of Creation and Innovation from Analysis of Ideas

It's impossible for those to happen at the same time, not just because multitasking is a myth but because your brain needs free rein to explore and discover to innovate. This can't happen if you are critiquing and judging your thoughts and words. You probably experienced this in the drawing exercise I asked you to do at the beginning of the book.

#2: Calm the Lizard Brain Down by Letting It Know the Analysis Is Coming After You Innovate

Sometimes that lizard brain just needs some assurance the safety net of judgment is coming. If you let your brain know the analysis is coming, it's more likely to be open to innovation and you'll even be more innovative in the filters you use to analyze.

Now, every time I run a meeting I take a page out of Cliff's playbook. I set expectations on the front end by letting people know the day is structured to innovation and analysis, just not at the same time. This approach also gives recognition to both sides of bringing ideas to fruition. You need to be able to go wide and innovate, and you need to be able to filter down and push the right ideas forward and the wrong ideas aside.

You don't need a three-hour meeting to incorporate both. If you have 10 minutes, spend six minutes innovating and four analyzing. If you have 30 minutes, spend 20 innovating and 10 analyzing. It's less about the time and more about structuring that time in a way that works for your brain. In doing this, you too will tap into Cliff's playbook and find that your results are measurably better.

Antennas Up

Join me for my friend's fortieth birthday as I take her to a dive bar in downtown Denver. We are hanging out, enjoying a few drinks, when the door blows open. Hit by a blast of cold air, I turn to see a pack of revelers dressed in various patterned Snuggies walking through the door. I'm so shocked by their appearance, I have to ask what's going on. I turn to the leader of the pack (I knew this because he had the most ornate of all the Snuggies) and

I ask him, "What are you guys doing?" In a way that only a drunk 20-something could respond, he yells, "It's a Snuggie bar crawl, wooooo!"

I give the leader of the pack a perplexed look, and he tells me these bar crawls are popular across the country and that most of his friends have done it.

What?! This campy infomercial that I am accosted with at two in the morning has gone from a cheesy infomercial to something hip and cool? This doesn't compute for me, not even after a few drinks. It's a blanket with holes in it. In my house, blankets with holes in them get thrown in the trash.

Did you know this blanket with holes in it sold more than 20 million units in 2010? I'm sure you've seen the infomercial or seen the Snuggie at a major retailer. You might even own one but are too embarrassed to admit it. I was for a long time.

And I'm sure you've had one of those moments, as I had in the bar, where you see something like the Snuggie bar crawl that makes your antenna perk up and think, *What??!!* In fact, those moments are all around you, but normally your head is so far down you shrug it off and move on. Whatever it is, it probably isn't important enough to pay attention to, and, without a doubt, it has zero relevance to your life.

What if the next time you have an "antennas up" moment, you stop and pay attention. What I saw that night wasn't some random, "who cares" thing. I caught a glimpse of a new product trend and behavior sweeping the country. I saw innovation in action.

There is a lot of relevant innovation going on out there if you pay attention. As you learned earlier, unlocking your style of Everyday Innovator will help you keep your antenna up.

Here's the experiment. For the next week, I want you to keep that antenna at attention, looking for interesting gems of innovation in your everyday life around you. While you are doing this, I want this question percolating in the back of your head: "How do I apply what I'm seeing right now to my world?"

Part of the challenge you face is seeing something innovative and filtering out the reticular activating system we discussed earlier because it doesn't see the relevancy. But if you continue to ask this question, your brain will help by seeking to find the relevancy for you. You don't even have to work too hard for it.

Begin tracking everything you see and how it may apply elsewhere in your encounters and activities. There is no need to judge, just keep track. If you are doing this solo, take stock of how many gems of innovation you find and all the ideas for your work and life they generate. If you are working in a team, each member should share their discoveries.

I start our monthly all-team check-in meetings by asking people to bring in one interesting product or experience and be prepared to tell everyone why it stood out to them. I do this because it keeps our antennas up. In one of these meetings, I brought in a T-shirt I kept seeing around town. It has a Jolly Roger (black with a white skull and crossbones) design except the skull is a cupcake. It is the iconic symbol of the lifestyle brand Johnny Cupcakes. I went on to explain that, after some research, I discovered this brand had some of the most loyal followers I'd ever seen—some even built shelving units to house their hundreds of Johnny Cupcakes T-shirts. The T-shirts are funky and irreverent, and founder Johnny Earle's videos give you a glimpse of an Everyday Innovator who is shaking things up.

The lightbulb goes off for Kelly, who is standing across from me in our meeting. She says, "How do we create a movement so meaningful our community loves being a part of it like Earle's customers love owning something as standard as a T-shirt?" And with that, the One Million Innovators challenge I shared with you in the Introduction was born.

All because we had our antennas up. If I had a headband for you with antennas, I would ask you to wear it the minute you wake up to the time you close your eyes. It's important you have them up 24/7—not for special occasions, not just when you think you have the energy to be innovative, but all the time.

As an Inquisitive Instinctual, your antenna will be full of questions and random connections. As a Fluid Tweaker, you'll see innovation in chaos and ways to improve just about anything. As an Experiential Risk Taker, you'll begin seeing innovation in the actions of others and in big chasms of opportunity. Whatever your Everyday Innovator style is, it lights up your antennas.

With your Everyday Innovator in action, antennas up, and that question percolating in the back of your mind, you'll discover a new world of insight and innovation.

Word Games

Looking at the same box, with the same questions, from the same perspective is going to get you nothing but the same answers. The challenge we often have in being Everyday Innovators is that we tackle our challenges and opportunities from the same starting point every time and that only takes us down the same path. As you've learned, your brain seeks efficiency, which is great in navigating routines of everyday life, such as driving to work and doing dishes, but it can hold you back from innovating.

This is where word games can help. You'll input new language, and that new language will take you down new paths. As you'll discover, even one word change can spark new thinking and new ideas. And as you change out words, you begin to use other words that speak to the different Everyday Innovator styles, like *bold* for Risk Takers or *create* for Imaginatives or *connect* for Instinctuals. For me, that's particularly exciting.

The way this experiment works is simple. You are going to write out your question, the one that represents the task, challenge, or opportunity you've been working on. It may look something like this:

How do we **stop** declining sales?
How do we **capture** the new target market?

After you've written that down, you are going to swap out the verb in the sentence. Using the opportunity statement above, swap out the word *capture* for other words.

What would it take to **develop** the new target market?
What would it take to **disrupt** the new target market?
What would it take to **build** the new target market?

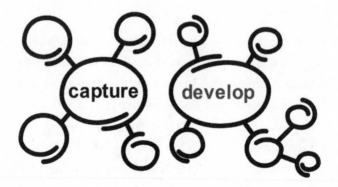

Mind-map ideas from each of those new sentences. This experiment reminds me of one of my favorite childhood games, Mad Libs, where a change in one word would completely shift the context of the entire sentence. The same applies here. Developing a target market is drastically different from capturing or disrupting. If you are doing this solo, use words that speak to your Everyday Innovator style. Go around the office and ask your colleagues for words to use. Broadening your input will broaden your results. The more tangential the language, the more innovative the ideas.

Reverse Engineer

Does it feel like that same challenge keeps rearing its ugly head? Like banging your head against the wall, trying to solve the same internal work flow issue, customer challenge, or ongoing market shift over and over again? The challenge you face is looking inward, into the constraints of your own world. It's when you remove those handcuffs and look purposefully outside your world that you find innovation.

In this experiment, I want you to first look laterally to your own category and then reverse engineer what they've done. Let's say you are a brand manager at a beauty company; perhaps you sell cosmetics—eye shadow, eyeliner, lipstick, etc. You are dealing with shrinking shelf space at the big box retailers, which means less visibility as your customers push their carts down the aisles.

To begin, write down your category and your challenge: beauty—declining shelf space and customer visibility.

Step One: Ask yourself who has the same challenge you do. In this case, that challenge is less visibility with your customers.

Step Two: List categories that have or did have this challenge. In this case, it could be close-in categories like hair products or clothing brands that are also dealing with less and less visibility as retail opportunities are decreasing with the closing of stores and the cluttering of space. It could be further-out categories like books, magazines, and even personal technology, like laptops, that are also dealing with the same challenges.

Step Three: List a few brands in those categories that you think have overcome the challenge in an innovative way. In this case, I might choose Moroccanoil for hair products because they are widely popular even though they aren't sold in traditional retail environments; Apple because they turned their retail space into an experience customers can't get enough of; and Burger King for being innovative in how they troll McDonald's (Google Burger King vs. McDonald's if you aren't aware of this phenomenon) and the competitive fast-food market to capture customers.

Step Four: This is where the magic happens as we reverse engineer what those companies did and apply it to your world. In the beauty category example, I might think the following:

Moroccanoil reverse engineer: They only place their products in salons, giving it a sense of value and sophistication. Their teal packaging is unique and eye-catching on the shelf. With my beauty brand, I need big retail, but perhaps I can create a stand-alone shelving unit that positions my brand in a different area, not next to the other brands. I'll use colors that are drastically different from the other beauty brands so customers can see it from across the store.

Apple reverse engineer: When you walk into an Apple store, it's like an interactive museum where you can play with everything. At the same time, it's almost minimalist in its design. With my beauty brand, do I remove all the informational charts and images to create a sleek look? Perhaps I can have a sample of everything for customers to play with, maybe even a makeup station where they can do a makeover on themselves before selecting a product.

Burger King: While most brands avoid their competitors, Burger King actively seeks out ways to jab at theirs, especially McDonald's. They even built an app that will award you a Whopper for a penny if you opened it while in a McDonald's and leave without making a purchase. With my beauty brand, what if we actively compared our products to the competitors, even doing makeover tutorials on YouTube with multiple brands?

In reading my beauty brand example, can you see how simple it is to innovate when you reverse engineer someone in a lateral category? The beauty of this exercise, pun intended, is that, again, it speaks directly to your Everyday Innovator style because you are most likely going to pick brands that speak to you and highlight examples that match as well. For example, as an Experiential Risk Taker, I might choose brands that go bold and try new things, even when it bucks the marketplace, like REI closing on Black Friday when everyone else is open.

This experiment is easy to do, and you'll be amazed how many industries and brands are struggling with the same challenges you are. If you are struggling with moving from the physical to the digital world, you might look at how music or books are marketed and sold. If you are struggling with building community with your customers, you might look at extreme sports and brands like Tough Mudder. If you are a local coffee shop trying to keep customers coming back, you might look at hotels and rewards programs. You get the picture. As you dig into this experiment, you'll discover a range of innovation that will spark innovative solutions in your world.

Look All Ways

"This is my favorite experiment. After we did this together,
I took the slide and placed it on my wall so that I'm always
reminded that there isn't just one path to innovation."

—Wendy Winter, Inquisitive Tweaker and
director at The Integer Group

To show you the value of this experiment, let's take five minutes to do the experiment together. I discourage you from taking a shortcut or reading through the entire exercise to see how it all comes together. If you do this step by step with me, you'll get an "aha" at the end that you can apply to everything you tackle.

Let's pick an everyday object for this experiment: a glass of water you can prepare in your kitchen. We are going to change this glass of water in different ways.

#1: Improve

Make the glass of water better. Perhaps the glass keeps the water a specific temperature or has a no-spill design, whatever would make it better for you.

#2: Create

Create a new use for this glass of water. Perhaps it's now a vase for flowers or an indicator of an earthquake by looking for ripples in the water; simply another use for the same object.

#3: Transform

Transform something else into a glass of water. Meaning, use a different object to accomplish the same objective—a holding vessel for water that you can drink out of, maybe a bowl or a hollowed-out piece of wood. Find a totally different object and transform it into this glass.

#4: Disrupt

Come up with the wildest, most disruptive, no-handcuffs innovation. Perhaps the glass self-fills, never needs to be washed, purifies the water, and can be used by astronauts because the water never leaves the glass unless you are drinking with your lips and it can recognize a particular set of lips. Go wild here.

#5: Worsen

Make the glass of water worse and then find a way to use it. Sounds weird, but go with me here. "Worse" might mean that the water is too dirty to drink. What can you do with dirty water? You can use it to irrigate your plants. Make it worse and then innovate against that.

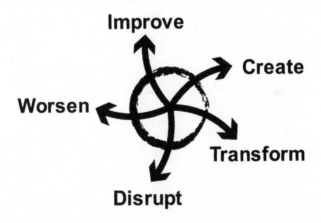

If you did this experiment with me, you now see how innovation isn't about taking one path to an answer, it's about exploring all the paths. In only exploring one path, we miss massive amounts of innovation and opportunity. What I find in doing this exercise with people is that the best innovation, the most meaningful solutions, often lie in a combination of answers we come up with to improve, create, transform, disrupt, and worsen. You will find the same, too. This experiment can be applied to a product, a service, a challenge, or an opportunity. If you are doing it solo, explore all of them. If you are with a team, either have everyone do all five or, as I often do with groups, assign teams to each one (one team improves, another transforms, etc.) and then share and build off your solutions. Not only is it fun, but it also opens up innovation paths not usually explored. And it's in that exploration that we find the most meaningful innovative solutions.

Chapter 15

Keeping Innovation Moving Forward

Different, Not Better

For a moment, think about the people, brands, and businesses you admire. Are they the ones that do it slightly better than someone else or are they the ones that dared to be different? I'm banking on the fact that it's the ones that do things differently. This is true for the people in our everyday lives and in the products and services we love and pay for.

One of my favorite opening questions for people I'm interviewing is "What's your favorite innovative person, brand, or business and why?" The answers range from people like movie director Quentin Tarantino and Zappos CEO Tony Hsieh to a favorite aunt who travels the world; to brands like Tesla, Southwest, Patagonia, and a neighborhood Ace Hardware that always has coffee and question of the day at the checkout. When I dig into why it's their favorite, the common theme is difference. "They aren't like everyone else," "They found a different way to do it," "They just get me in a way others don't," "They are true to who they are and I love that."

Not better, different. We call them rebels, mavericks, and instigators, but they are just Everyday Innovators like you and me that embrace their uniqueness. What makes you different is what makes you unique. It's what makes you think, act, make decisions, behave, choose, and communicate in your way.

Here's the challenge. In today's crazy-cluttered, fast-paced, hypercompetitive world, being better isn't enough. This is true at the personal and the business level. I call it the "ER" trap—bettER, strongER, fastER, smartER…you get the point. The challenge is someone can come along and out-"ER" you at any moment. It's not that hard. You are probably thinking about how to out-ER someone right now. I know someone is thinking about how to do that to you, too.

The cereal aisle at the grocery store is a prime example. It's cluttered, everything looks the same, I can't remember which brand is which or who said what. As in life, there is limited space and attention so everyone is trying to be louder and better than the options next to it. Frankly, I do my best to tune out most of what I see and get through the cereal shopping experience as fast as possible. Why? Because the entire aisle has fallen into the ER trap.

More fiber
With extra fiber
10% more fiber
12% more fiber
15% more fiber
15% more fiber and vitamins
20% more fiber and essential vitamins
25% more fiber, essential vitamins, delicious original taste

It just keeps going, with one cereal product trying to out-better the next. I shake my head every time I have to go down the breakfast aisle. Sorry, cereal manufacturers, but do you really think I'm stopping, comparing all the packages, and making my decision based on a few more grams of fiber? Of course not. You, the reader, probably glazed over reading the list here—and these are only the claims I can remember.

This is also what I think we start to sound like when we try to sound more like each other and out-better one another. I can see people in the room start to tune out when we all start to sound the same. I do it, too.

We are tribal in nature and that means we do our best to try to fit in. We want to be accepted into the tribe because, in the old days, not being accepted meant being banished, and banished meant no protection from the elements and no food. But we forget that for a tribe to really work we need all different types of people and skills—gardeners, hunters, builders, fixers, storytellers, etc. Your tribe today doesn't need you to be like them. Can you imagine what would have happened if a tribe was filled with only hunters or only storytellers? There'd be no gardeners to grow food, no shelters to sleep in. In your tribe today, would anything get done if everyone knew how to build a product but nobody knew how to get it into stores? Or if everyone at your architecture firm knew one approach to building parking lots but nobody knew how to build a house? What if everyone on your team was an Inquisitive or a Risk Taker? Would you see things through?

Your tribe needs you to bring your unique set of skills. Your tribe needs you to show up as "you," not them. Your differentiated set of skills is what makes you a highly valued member of your tribe.

As I write this book, the music artist Lizzo isn't rising to incredible fame and popularity by being like all the other music out there. You would recognize her songs the minute you heard them. She shows up with her personality, her style, and her incredible vocal chords, and she's inherently different from all the other artists out there.

You can do the same whether you are Sally in account management in marketing; Enrique, a client relations director in cyber security; or Rondell, the franchise owner.

It's essential that you don't find yourself stuck in the ER trap. Don't do better, do different. And different is who you already are. It's your unique Everyday Innovator style layered onto your one-of-a-kind personality. That's how you show up as different. That's how you have a stronger voice. It's not by sounding similar to everyone else; it's by sounding like your most awesome, innovative self.

Better Isn't Enough. To Win, You Need to Be Different.

Speaking is a big part of my job as a business owner, so several years back I joined an association for people in the public speaking business. My first in-person meeting was also book swap day. Most of the one hundred members in attendance had books piled up on a table by the registration desk. As you can imagine, people in the business of communication are very welcoming and were actively greeting me as I made my way through the room. With each interaction I was told, "If you want to be a speaker, you need to write a book," or, "If you don't have a book, no one will hire you," or, "If you want to be taken seriously, you need to have a book." I started to worry that I wasn't ready to pursue more speaking engagements without a book to prove my worth.

As the meeting started and I took my seat, I caught a glimpse of the table of books that was now spilling onto the registration desk. I will always remember in that moment thinking, *If the hundreds of members here all have books and the thousands of speakers, aka my competitors, have books, and we are all sending them to the same people, how am I supposed to stand out?*

In that moment the idea for something I called "creative-tees" was born. T-shirts with innovative statements on them. While everyone else was sending the traditional one-page marketing sheet and a book, I sent a media sizzle kit along with a "creative-tee." We had a phenomenal hire rate that year.

Clearly, I'm not saying that writing a book is bad. If you have something of value to share, you should definitely write a book. I am saying that in the competitive landscape we live in, different wins.

It's why this book is not just a list of personality descriptions and hyperboles and includes real-world stories and access to an online assessment and tool kit. My goal isn't to be better than your other reading options, it is to be different in a meaningful way. The hamster wheel of better exhausts you, but different keeps you moving forward.

Take Small Steps

Heather Kluter had a big vision. As an Inquisitive Risk Taker she wanted to challenge the norm and bring drastic innovation to how the company approached innovation, or in her mind, the lack of it, by creating an innovation center of excellence. But she worked at Hyundai, a company that had built its success on formality and structure. Heather knew if she went to her boss to ask for millions of dollars for this wild idea, she'd get nowhere. Instead, Heather did what we never talk about in innovation—she took some small steps. First, she asked for a few hours to take some field trips to look for concepts that would improve their cars. A field trip turned into allocating a day to innovation. A day turned into a team, and, after a few years of baby steps in the right direction, Heather was standing in an innovation center where employees from across the globe could come, innovate, and then bring that innovation back to their teams.

Sometimes, to go big and bold you have to be small and cautious. If you are willing and have the ability to leap big, though, I'll hand you an energy drink and pat you on the back before you leap. Most of our realities, however, especially in large organizations, include layers of bureaucracy that need to be broken down one step at a time. Heather reminds us there is a lot of power in, as she calls it, "assertive grace" and baby steps.

Figure out your big end game, and break it down into baby steps that will get you to your goal.

Chapter 16

Avoid Launch & Abandon

Before we sail off to the seas of innovation, there is one more pitfall to learn to avoid: the frustrations of launch and abandon. While we have covered being a high-performing team, I am zeroing in on launch and abandon from an individual Everyday Innovator perspective so you can ensure you stay innovative. Innovation is about people. If you want to ignite, sustain, and scale innovation, you must ensure you innovate and allow the people around you to do so as well. When you unlock the innovation inside yourself and those around you, the culture will follow. The key to innovation isn't in the process or the system, it's in the people—people like you.

Teams and tribes, after all, are a collection of individuals seeking to innovate, contribute, and be heard. If you can help yourself and those around you to avoid launch and abandon behavior and put into place some of the team elements I mentioned, such as Complete Feedback Loop and Experimentation, you'll discover that innovation is ever flowing and ever present in your work and life.

All Engines Go

All engines are a go; the innovation rocket lifts off; you propel upward with speed and momentum. Then, just as you are really moving, hitting outer space, something happens. You shut down the fires and send your innovation rocket in a spiraling free fall back to Earth. This is what I call launch and abandon.

I see it all the time. The excitement is palpable and the commitment to innovation is at an all-time high. You are psyched up to put what you've learned into action. You get a good start and then work and life "take over." Someone shuts you down, for whatever reason, and suddenly the innovation fires flame out. The worst part about launch and abandon is that you falsely prove to yourself you aren't innovative. "See, it's proof it didn't work." What didn't work is not your ability to innovate; you didn't have the proper fuel to keep the fires going when there were internal and external pressures that wanted you to burn out.

One of the first things you have to do is squelch self-doubt.

Squelching Self-Doubt

When that oversize envelope from University of California Berkeley arrived, I was stunned. How did I get in? The truth is I wasn't the best academically, and I struggled with the traditional learning model in high school. I was that student the teachers found disruptive and annoying. I went to junior college first, where my desire to get the heck out of my hometown pushed me to do better and apply to Berkeley. I never imagined I'd get in. In fact, I didn't believe it until well into the first semester.

I was sure the letter was meant for someone else, so I called admissions to confirm this letter wasn't for a different Tamara Ghandour. I only packed two suitcases because I was sure I would be sent home the minute they realized I was an imposter, not the Tamara they were expecting. On my first day of classes, I was so convinced that I wasn't supposed to be there that I sat in the back of the classroom. That way, when the professor did the initial roll call, no one would notice I didn't say "Here" if my name wasn't called.

The worst of my insecurities about being inadequate and average compared to the other students at this top-tier school came in a very intimate setting. The main anthropology class had more than two hundred students, so we also had to attend weekly study groups led by graduate students. There were about six students in each study group. Every week, one of us would be given the homework of leading the class in what we thought the lesson or insights were in the week's chapter. This particular week was my turn. If memory serves me, the chapter was about how different cultures across the globe had different perspectives and values when confronted with the same object or situation. (Funny how this comes full circle given what I do now.)

I was nervous and wanted so badly to get it right, to look smart. I wanted everyone in the room to know I belonged. I read and reread the chapter at least 20 times. I wrote down my thoughts, scratched them out, rewrote them. I overanalyzed and undervalued everything I wrote. I doubted myself at every turn. This was my chance to prove to everyone I was smart enough to play with the big dogs...and I was failing miserably. Finally, after late nights of self-doubt and frustration, I landed on what I thought would be the right answer, the one the graduate student teacher was looking for.

I walked in, presented my case, and was instantly met with disappointment. The graduate student leading the class looked at me with surprise. He very easily explained why my answer was way off base and went on to lead the class in the real discussion.

I was heartbroken. The worst part is the answer he shared was the one I knew was right but had scratched out because I didn't think I could possibly get the answer that quickly or effortlessly. I was so focused on proving myself that I completely undervalued and second-guessed what I brought to the table. I left that class in tears.

That feeling of lacking worthiness has always stuck with me.

It's even hard writing this story because it conjures a lot of those old feelings. Sometimes I catch myself falling back into that place of doubt. When I'm meeting with a big client or interviewing someone famous, that little voice I call Bernard says, *Who are you to be here?* and *Be quiet or they will realize you aren't as smart as they are.* I have to continually convince myself that I bring tremendous value and worth.

And so do you. I'm opening up and sharing this story with you because I want you to see all that self-doubt you carry around is self-inflicted BS that is doing more harm than good. You aren't alone; it's perfectly normal even for the seemingly most successful people, and shedding it is solely up to you—an inside job. You have to believe you are the one bringing the value to the table. With this book, I hope you'll have gained the knowledge and the tools to do so with ease.

Launch and abandon can be avoided by the mental and social armor you acquired through reading this book. The three techniques described here: death by a thousand cuts, NOT; you don't need 10,000 hours; and jump on two, will help you, the Everyday Innovator you now are, to fight the internal and external pressures that cause you to abandon your mission.

#1: Death by a Thousand Cuts, NOT

Lingchi loosely translates to "death by a thousand cuts" and was a particularly brutal form of torture in ancient China. It was a long and drawn-out process whereby a person would receive small cuts on the skin. Each cut in itself was hardly noticeable, but, over time, and with enough of these cuts, they resulted in a slow, painful death. The point wasn't to inflict immediate pain or death, but to see how long a person could endure before losing consciousness or dying.

In modern times, psychologists use the term "death by a thousand cuts" to refer to the way a major change can be accepted as a normal situation if it happens slowly, through unnoticeable increments of change.

Think of "death by a thousand cuts" as the fractional little moments of negative jabs and comments from doubters. Can you feel the tiny tug on your sleeve trying to hold you down as you rise? Often they go unnoticed or are brushed off as small incidents, but over time they wear you down, killing your spirit. And the jabs don't come from your enemies, the ones from whom you know you'll face resistance. They come from those closest to you.

A few years ago, I was extremely unhealthy. Writing that doesn't sound that bad, but the truth is, I was eating cupcakes almost every day. Although, if you asked me at the time, I would blame my inability to lose weight on my post-kid metabolism. My idea of exercise was to go to the gym, get on a few machines, look as if I was working hard; maybe jump on a treadmill, where I didn't last long. I'd cap it off by eating a big ol' burrito on the way home. Even more ridiculous, I used to get my favorite peanut butter chocolate candy at the grocery checkout, eat it in the car, and throw away the wrapper before I walked into the house. If no one saw me eat it, the calories didn't count, right?

Fast forward several years and I've not only lost 35 pounds, but I now have actual muscles. My cupboards are cleaned out of most (I do have two kids) bad-for-you foods, and I'm drinking water faster than I can refill my water bottle. Some might call my fit lifestyle an annoying obsession.

What does my obsession with lifting heavy weights and an insane move called thrusters have to do with your journey to becoming a rock star innovator? Let me explain. When my second child was in elementary school, a neighborhood CrossFit gym hosted a free family night on school grounds. I thought my kids would love it, so I went with them one summer evening. We rolled on the ground, jumped over cones, swung light kettle bells. I thought, *What's all the buzz about, this isn't so bad.* And with a false sense of confidence, I signed up for the real CrossFit class.

My first day was a one-on-one fitness assessment with the gym manager, Whitney. All we did were some air squats, knee push-ups, and pull-ups with a very thick band…and I wanted to die. I couldn't actually sign up that day because I was on the verge of throwing up and needed to leave before embarrassing myself. I was faced with the cold, hard truth. The powerful, strong, mentally tough person that was me on the inside did not match the soft, out-of-shape quitter on the outside. The full realization was that this was true across many aspects of my life, not just fitness. I went to bed that night feeling miserable and excited at the same time. I signed up that week and began a journey of testing my mental and physical limits. Again, this story isn't about how fit I am, or how fit you are, it's about what happens when you make a decision to elevate your game.

As soon as the new me emerged, I expected extreme accolades from everyone I knew, not because I needed validation or even cared what others thought of me; I just figured when you bring your A game, people would see that and be motivated to raise their game—or at least proud of me for doing so. The exact opposite happened. What I discovered was death by a thousand cuts. As it turns out, when you elevate your game and unleash your superpowers into the world, it acts as a shining mirror to others' mediocrity.

It started when I was walking my kiddos to school one chilly fall morning with a few of the other neighborhood parents. I had already woken up, had two cups of coffee, got my workout in, and even answered a few emails before the 7:35 a.m. walk commenced. I was feeling pretty proud of myself as I strutted out the door, still in workout gear. I met up with the other parents. Then they lowered the boom. One of them asked if I was still being crazy and getting up at 4:00 a.m. or if that phase had passed. As I humbly answered yes, I felt the first cut. One by one, the other parents chimed in, adding their cuts.

"It's crazy, Tamara. You should sleep every now and again."

"I would never want to do that."

"Aren't you too old to be lifting heavy weights and doing all that fancy stuff anyway?"

"You know you are going to injure yourself soon. You should try walking, it's safer."

I started that walk standing tall and proud; by the time we walked the two and a half blocks to school, I was slumped over, questioning my judgment. This happened every morning for a few weeks.

I started questioning their lack of support. Why would people who are supposed to be in my corner do that to me? The answer is relatively obvious: because performing at your peak will initially bring out the insecurity in those who would rather play a mediocre game. To be fair, I don't think they realize they are doing it. They are simply trying to pull you down back to where it's safe and comfortable. You'll encounter it from the people you least expect. Don't be surprised.

During your innovative growth process, you may be taunted by death-by-a-thousand-cuts comments like:

"Hey! Let's not go overboard here!"

"Geez, Beatrice, way to make the rest of us look bad."

"I appreciate the wild thinking, but we can't do that."

"Let's not get ahead of ourselves."

"Oh, that's just you thinking your crazy thoughts."

Like death by a thousand cuts, comments like that on their own may even go unnoticed, but over the course of time they are an innovation killer.

Don't let them get to you. Instead, stand tall in your innovator rock star status.

With every walk to school, I stood strong. Over time, they not only stopped discouraging me, but several stepped up into their own fitness routines. I am so proud of them.

But this story isn't about getting fit, it's about staying strong in being your best self and not letting the magnetic pull of mediocre drag you down. Don't let those living in fear pull you back to their "misery loves company" place.

Fortunately, you can easily avoid death by a thousand cuts by doing two things:

Recognize them for what they are. Someone's insecurities and jealousy at your newfound level of performance. Seeing them for what they are will keep you from getting cut. You become

Teflon—that material used to make nonstick cookware—
put-downs slide right off.

Bring them along for the journey. You now have the knowledge
you need to figure out how to get them to an innovative space.
As I've mentioned throughout these pages, it's your responsibility.
And the more innovators, the stronger the web. These pages provide techniques for how to speak to others in a way that unlocks
their innovative mind, how to trigger them in a way that is moti-
vating. You even have an assessment they can take to show them
how they can become their best selves, too.

As a friend once said to me when I was starting to slump over
after weeks of being jabbed, "Straighten out your crown and stand
tall, Tamara. Eventually, they'll get tired of looking up, and they'll
straighten up, too, so they can meet you eye to eye."

You'll find this is true when you unlock your rock star innovator. That's why it's so helpful to be surrounded by others also
unleashing their rock star innovators. It creates an unbreakable
web of innovation. And if you are starting out alone, there's no
need to worry. The more you innovate, the more your energy will
become infectious to those around you. You doing your thing will
have a massive positive impact on those around you.

#2: You Don't Need 10,000 Hours

In Malcom Gladwell's book *Outliers: The Story of Success,* he talks
about the fact that it takes 10,000 hours of practice to become an
expert at something. I agree with him, but fortunately you aren't
learning a new skill, so you don't need that many hours to be a
leading Everyday Innovator. You are naturally skilled in being
innovative even though your innovation muscles may be weak and

dusty after years of inactivity. You need practice to wake them up. It doesn't happen overnight, and it definitely doesn't happen if you wait for that one special moment.

I turned the dial to a Beatles music marathon while driving to work one day. The Beatles, while really the music of my parents, are worth a few minutes on the radio. The songs were punctuated by interviews with Paul McCartney. During one particular interview break, the host asked McCartney what it felt like when they landed their first big record deal, and if he felt an intense pressure to be creative and come up with new songs. McCartney responded by sharing that by the time they got to their first recording session they could have recorded eight hours' worth of songs. The Beatles had been practicing and playing live for a long time before they got their big break—late-night shows, empty bars, unpaid gig after unpaid gig.

You don't need 10,000 hours to become an Everyday Innovator, but you do need to step up and practice every chance you get. If you are a Risk Taker, this may mean practicing by speaking up in that mostly pointless Monday meeting, so when you get to the big everything-on-the-line moment, you are ready. If you are an Imaginative, it may mean playing around with new possibilities on low-risk tasks, so you are firing on all cylinders when you are asked to join the team on that new initiative. Check the charts in this book that will help you practice.

Don't let the need for perfection or the pressure to go from novice to expert overnight stop you. Remember, practice doesn't make perfect, it makes progress.

#3: Jump on Two

My girlfriend and I were rattling along a Costa Rican highway in our rented, ratty old Jeep. I think by the time we rented it, the Jeep was more duct tape than metal. As we were driving, we both saw it. A hand-painted sign on a torn-up old cardboard box, propped up against a rock. It said, "Bungee Jumping Next Right."

We veered off the highway, onto the dirt roads, and followed the cardboard arrows nailed to trees until we came to the rusty abandoned bridge, spanning a very deep ravine. We pulled up at the same time as another pair of tourists, clearly craving some off-the-beaten-path adventure.

We all got out of our Jeeps in our lightweight matching travel gear and headed to the weathered shack to check in. We then made our way to the bridge overlooking the very deep ravine with trickles of water winding between ginormous boulders. A nice young man with a pearly white smile and a heap of cords tangled at his feet looked at us and said, "Who wants to go first?"

I stood there tongue-tied, looking alternately over the railing and back at my fellow travelers. Let's just say I didn't argue when the others agreed to go first. One by one, I watched as they leapt off the bridge with sheer terror shot across their faces. To my surprise, each came up with the look of total joy in their smiles.

Then it was my turn. I don't remember most of the preparation—our guide Velcroing the straps to my ankles and attaching those straps to the bridge. I must have blanked out and came to as I was being hoisted onto the ledge with nothing to hold on to. My legs were shaking and my heart was beating so hard and fast, I'm sure it was visible through my shirt. I was numb with fear.

I heard the nice young man say, "On the count of three, you are going to jump up and away from the bridge."

Okay, go on three, got it, I thought. He started to count: one...two...and I jumped.

I couldn't wait one more second. If I had waited one more second, I would have jumped back down to the safety of the bridge.

But when my feet left the railing and I was soaring through the air, I went from living in fear to living in freedom. I have never felt anything so liberating and exhilarating.

As I was lifted back to the bridge that day, I promised myself I would never forget that one second between two and three. It takes one second for you to go from "What if" to "Now what." It takes one second for you to brush your brilliance under a rug. It takes one second for you to talk yourself out of doing the thing you know is right.

How many times have you been on the ledge of a decision and talked yourself out of it? How often have you backtracked on an idea because it was too bold, so you played it safe and watered it down? That one second is the difference between leaping and falling back to safety.

The voice I hear in my head, the one that keeps me moving forward, the voice I want you to hear in your head is, *jump on two*.

With this, I've brought you full circle, identifying innovation as it relates to you; how you impact and participate in your teams and your teams with you; how you avoid pitfalls on your path; how to be a leader who can tap into the best everyone has to offer; using your triggers to move in your best directions; and avoiding the biggest stopper of all when you're ready to launch.

Go on, have the courage to ***jump on two***.

Notes

Introduction

1. Dana Wilde. *Train Your Brain: How to Build a Million Dollar Business in Record Time* (Carlsbad, CA: Balboa Press, 2013), p. 61.
2. "Study Reveals Global Creativity Gap," Adobe, April 23, 2012; adobe.com/aboutadobe/pressroom/pressreleases/201204/042312AdobeGlobal CreativityStudy.html.

Chapter 1

1. Erik L. Westby and V.L. Dawson "Creativity: Asset or Burden in the Classroom?" *Creativity Research Journal*, vol. 8, no. 1, pp. 1–10; DOI: 10.1207 /s15326934crj0801_ https://doi.org/10.1207/s15326934crj0801_1.
2. Don Joseph Goewey. "85% of What We Worry about Never Happens," *HuffPost*, August 25, 2015; huffpost.com/entry/85-of-what-we-worry -about_b_8028368?ncid=engmodushpmg00000004.

Chapter 2

1. Heidi Grant Halvorson, PhD. "Longer May Not Be Better, but It Seems That Way," *Psychology Today*, February 16, 2011; psychologytoday.com /za/blog/the-sciencesuccess/201102/longer-may-not-be-better-it-seems -way?amp.
2. Ibid.
3. Stéphane Garelli. "Why You Will Probably Live Longer than Most Big Companies," IMD, December 2016; imd.org/research-knowledge /articles/why-you-will-probably-live-longer-than-most-big-companies/.
4. Thomas Friedman. The Aspen Institute's Resnick Action Forum, August 7, 2017; youtube.com/watch?time_continue=7&v=GyZHySRUKXI.

5. Richard E - Bailey. "There Are Now 5 Generations in the Workforce—Can They Work Together?" *Fast Company,* February 2, 2019; fastcompany.com/90302569/there-are-now-5-generations-in-the-workforce-can-they-work-together?partner=rss&utm_source=rss&utm_medium=feed&utm_campaign=rss+fastcompany&utm_content=rss?cid=search.
6. *Wall Street Journal.* "Discussing the Era of 'New Collar Workers' with IBM CEO Ginni Rommety," WSJ Video, January 24, 2019; wsj.com/video/discussing-the-era-of-new-collar-workers-with-ibm-ceo-ginni-rometty/8865662F-6180-4312-918C-DE47856E1DA8.html.
7. McKinsey Global Institute. "Jobs Lost, Jobs Gained: What the Future of Work Will Mean for Jobs, Skills and Wages," November 2017 report; mckinsey.com/featured-insights/future-of-work/jobs-lost-jobs-gained-what-the-future-of-work-will-mean-for-jobs-skills-and-wages.

Chapter 3

1. Levi Buchanan. "From Janitor to Superstar," IGN, May 10, 2012; ign.com/articles/2009/09/10/from-janitor-to-superstar.

Chapter 4

1. American Psychology Association. "Speaking of Psychology: The Neuroscience of Creativity," APA, episode 10; accessed June 10, 2019; apa.org/research/action/speaking-of-psychology/neuroscience-creativity.
2. Roger E. Beaty, et al. "Robust Prediction of Individual Creative Ability from Brain Functional Connectivity," Harvard University, Department of Psychology, July 31, 2017.
3. Bogdan, Draganski, et al. "Changes in Grey Matter Induced by Training," *Nature,* vol. 427, January 2004, pp. 311–12.
4. Stephanie Liou. "Neuroplasticity," Hopes Huntington's Outreach Project for Education, Stanford University, June 6, 2010; hopes.stanford.edu/neuroplasticity/#strategies-for-promoting-brain-reorganization.
5. Francisco Saez. "How to Beat Your 'Lizard Brain,'" *FacileThings*; accessed July 5, 2019; facilethings.com/blog/en/lizard-brain.

Chapter 7

1. Sam Biddle. "Ten Greatest (Accidental) Inventions of All Time: Sometimes Genius Arrives Not by Choice—but by Chance," NBC News; accessed June 15, 2019; nbcnews.com/id/38870091/ns/technology_and

_science-innovation/t/greatest-accidental-inventions-all-time
/#.XXwBh5NKjBJ.
2. "Penicillin: An Accidental Discovery Changed the Course of Medicine,"
   Endocrine Today, August 2008; healio.com/endocrinology/news/print
   /endocrine-today/%7B15afd2a1-2084-4ca6-a4e6-7185f5c4cfb0%7D
   /penicillin-an-accidental-discovery-changed-the-course-of-medicine.
3. Ibid.

Chapter 9

1. David Rock and Heidi Grant. "Why Diverse Teams Are Smarter," *Harvard Business Review,* November 4, 2016; hbr.org/2016/11/why-diverse
   -teams-are-smarter.
2. Alison Reynolds and David Lewis. "Teams Solve Problems Faster When
   They're More Cognitively Diverse," *Harvard Business Review,* March 30, 2017;
   hbr.org/2017/03/teams-solve-problems-faster-when-theyre-more-cognitively
   -diverse.
3. Michael Schneider. "Google Spent 2 Years Studying 180 Teams. The Most
   Successful Ones Shared These 5 Traits," *Inc.,* July 19, 2007; inc.com/
   michael-schneider/google-thought-they-knew-how-to-create-the-perfect.
   html.

Chapter 11

1. Matthew Daddona. "Got Milk? How the Iconic Campaign Came to Be,
   25 Years Ago," *Fast Company,* June 13, 2018; fastcompany.com/40556502
   /got-milk-how-the-iconic-campaign-came-to-be-25-years-ago.
2. Ibid.

Chapter 13

1. "Tough Mudder Facts & Trivia," Tough Mudder; accessed August 1,
   2019; mudder-guide.com/guide/tough-mudder-facts-and-trivia/#history.
2. Ray Dalio. *Principles: Life and Work* (New York: Simon & Schuster, 2017),
   pp. 81–94.

Chapter 14

1. Kevin McSpadden. "You Now Have an Attention Span Shorter than a Gold-
   fish," *Time,* May 14, 2015; time.com/3858309/attention-spans-goldfish/.

2. E. Garcia-Rill. "Reticular Activating System," *Encyclopedia of Neuroscience*, 2009; sciencedirect.com/topics/neuroscience/reticular-activating-system.

3. K. C. Cole. "Brain's Use of Shortcuts Can Be a Route to Bias: Perception: The Mind Relies on Stereotypes to Make Fast Decisions. But in Hiring, That Can Lead to Discrimination," *Los Angeles Times*, May 1, 1995; latimes.com/archives/la-xpm-1995-05-01-mn-61017-story.html.

4. April Perry. "Want to Calm Your Mind? Close the Open Loop," *Learn Do Become,* July 18, 2016; learndobecome.com/want-to-calm-your-mind -close-the-open-loops/.

Index

About the Author

© Laura Mahoney Photography

The impact of Tamara's break-through work on human-centric innovation can be seen in individuals, teams, and organizations across the globe. As the creator of the proprietary Innovation Quotient Edge (IQE) assessment and the president of LaunchStreet Consultancy, Tamara has helped tens of thousands gain the competitive edge by unlocking the power of innovation. With 25 plus years of work experience, Tamara knows what it takes to truly drive innovation, relevancy, and value in an ever-changing, complex world.

Through a unique combination of neuroscience, brain mechanics, behavioral and social psychology and work experience, Tamara brings it all together through real-world insights and lessons, making innovation accessible and tangible for everyone. Tamara is a sought after keynote speaker and advisor due to her unique ability to make innovation personal and actionable. Tamara developed the IQE assessment, the only tool that helps people discover their unique Everyday Innovator style, so they can bring out the best in themselves and the best in those around them. For many leaders and teams, it is the secret sauce for igniting their peak performance and developing high-performing teams that innovate and win.

Tamara's company, LaunchStreet, is the go-to innovation partner for companies like Arrow Electronics, Schneider Electric, Red Robin, RICOH and US Army Research Labs when they want to create a culture of innovation that wins and develop innovative solutions for their biggest challenges. Her IQE system has helped ignite, scale and sustain innovation inside and out organizations of all sizes. Most importantly her work helps everyone realize their innovation capabilities and apply it daily.

At 27 she was the youngest person ever named to leadership in a leading global advertising agency. If you've walked the aisles of Target you've pushed your cart past products and brands that have benefited from Tamara's innovative approach – everything from Cheerios and Johnsonville Sausage to Procter & Gamble and Clorox. She has run multi-million dollar businesses and launched a few of her own, learning from her successes and, most importantly, her failures. Tamara has been featured on the TODAY SHOW, EO FIRE Podcast, the New York Times, Denver Business Journal, NBC 9News and on radio stations across the country. As a kid in computer camp, Tamara won the "I'll try anything once" award - a motto she still lives by.